PROMO POWER SUPREMACY

THE QUICK AND EASY, NO-NONSENSE GUIDE
TO GETTING NOTICED, BUILDING
RELATIONSHIPS AND GROWING
YOUR COMPANY USING
PROMOTIONAL
PRODUCTS

MO YUSUFF

PROMO POWER SUPREMACY

WHAT READERS ARE SAYING ABOUT PROMO POWER SUPREMACY

It'd be easy to assume that Mo wrote this book just to drum up new business. And, of course, he's hoping it will because that is one of his aims.

But here's the thing. His MAIN aim is to help business owners just like me to get real value from promotional marketing products. This shows right from the very first chapter of his book.

If you're anything like me — a one-woman powerhouse of a business — you're aware there's no such thing as a 'marketing budget'. We need every penny we spend to work hard and we need it to bring a measurable return — or we need to see it's not working so we can ditch it and try something else.

Mo knows that too, and he wants his clients to get as much ROI as possible from working with him... even if that means he doesn't do quite as well as he could in the short-term. Because unlike some other promo companies I've crossed paths with in the past, Mo wants to build long-term relationships with his clients.

This book is just the first step on that journey, and I wish he'd written it years ago.

Starting with the 7 Reasons Why Most Promotional Products Fail Miserably, and How to Fix That, the book is packed full of useful and practical stuff to help us avoid the pitfalls of promo marketing. And Chapter 2 is just brilliant: it'll be a revelation to most business owners.

Mo's also included a chapter about how he and other businesses have successfully used lumpy mail and promotional products to get real, tangible results. There are a bunch of good ideas in there for us to swipe and adapt.

And he also goes in-depth regarding how to create and run a whole marketing system — including where the real profits lie, and how to dig them out.

If you run your own business, I strongly recommend you read this book. There's no nonsense in there. No fads. No thinly disguised sales pitches.

It's packed full of valuable, timeless, practical stuff you can put to work straightaway. And it's a good read. Enjoy!

Vicky Fraser -
www.businessforsuperheroes.com

Well, in this book, Mo tells you upfront and honestly why bad or poorly thought-out promotional products don't work and why they have such a bad rap. But he also gives you a blueprint for how appealing and well thought-out promotional products can work for your business and, what's more, work exceptionally well.

I used Mo to source and produce a promotional product for one of my businesses, which I used for a campaign to bring lapsed clients back into the fold.

But it wasn't just the product itself that made the sales, it was the information that Mo shares with you inside this book on how to use them in a campaign. And that is where the gold is. And that's not something that many people in his industry will share with you.

In addition, Mo gives you a wealth of information into the motivation and buying habits of your potential clients, and armed with that knowledge (and Mo's products), you are bound to hit the marketing sweet spot.

Mo has put the hard work into creating the perfect marketing campaign using promotional products so you don't have to. All you have to do is read this book.

Kat Smith of Kat Smith Success Systems Ltd
www.growyoursalonfast.com

 *I have known Mo for a couple of years. In fact, we catch up almost every week on Skype to talk business and help each other in our respective journeys.*

Mo knows what he is talking about, not only when it comes to promotional products, but when it comes to marketing in general. He is not an armchair expert, rather, he has a rich experience in implementing everything he teaches you in 'Promo Power Supremacy'.

If you are a business owner or work in marketing, you'd be a fool if you didn't follow Mo's advice.

Mark Cottle of Frontline Premier Offshore Services
http://frontlinephilippines.com/

 *You may well ask: what exactly is the point of spending a good portion of your limited marketing resources on promotional products?*

Does it actually work for your business?

Well, it's about time someone explained the facts for you. This has now been done in 'Promo Power Supremacy' by Mo Yusuff.

I first met Mo over 20 years ago when his company became our garment supplier and printer. I was very intrigued when he said he was going to publish a book on a subject that was close to both his heart and mine.

This is the world we work within. We both run companies that produce, print, distribute, design, market and sell custom branded products. Our client profiles span the whole spectrum, from the small one-person businesses, to global corporations. Our customers are all different but the process we implement is the same for each and every one, big or small.

If you are in the business of marketing then you really should read 'Promo Power Supremacy'. Within 7 chapters, Mo takes you through multiple tried and tested processes that you need to put in place if you really want to grow your business with promotional products. It's no quick fix. In fact, it's bloody hard work, but once you have implemented the procedures outlined in this book, you will see the benefits.

It's no great secret that a lot of branded business gifts are badly chosen, cheap and unrepresentative of the company whose brand they carry. More often than not, they are given out to the wrong people and ultimately end up in the bin, unused and unloved.

Please do not make the same mistakes we see time and time again. Get it right first time and incorporate them into a strategy that works.

We know that with the right advice and a good promotional product partner, you can reach the new customers that your company needs in order to grow and evolve. And most importantly, Mo will show you how to keep those customers loyal to you and make them come back again and again.

I know how much hard work has gone into developing these strategies and getting them all down on paper and into this book. It's the distillation of many years of experience, from trial and error to the incorporation of modern marketing techniques that makes this book a real winner.

You could say that this book is a great addition to your marketing strategy, whatever your business background.

I'm confident it will help you grow your business and, once again, Mo has delivered a perfect gift that you will most definitely want to keep.

Richard Sullivan of Navillus Print Gifts limited
www.print-gifts.com

 This book covers so much more than buying promotional products, such as pens and keyrings, to give to your customers. It is a marketing blueprint for finding the right clients, coming up with ideas on how to keep them as clients and how to get lapsed clients to come back to you.

Chapter 4 includes a complete marketing campaign, which you can use to find the best customers in your target market.

There are loads of take away points/tips throughout to help you.

So, if you are looking for ideas, tips and strategies to help you grow your business then invest in this book.

Robert Cartoon of Cartoon Consultancy

This is more than a book on just 'promotional products'... I mean, first and foremost, it delivers on that promise – it details exactly why you should use promotional products and how they can be used to grow your business. But more than that, it gives you why you should be using promotional products at all... whether it's to reinforce your brand or be the core focus of a marketing campaign.

After reading this book several things should be true: the first is that you will be armed with knowledge on why you should use promotional products with your marketing (and what ones to use), but, more importantly, how you should use them. Second, you should understand marketing at a deeper level than thinking it's just about sending a product off in the post to 'get out there'. Third, you should be more familiar with specific strategies, which can absolutely transform your business if you take action and get on and do it. Finally, you'll understand just why there are thousands upon thousands of poor quality promotional products out there that could end up making you look poor quality – and how to avoid them.

There aren't many books out there that go into this much detail on how to structure a marketing campaign. To have this one, combined with the promotional products aspect, makes it a fiercely good read indeed and something that every business owner should read at least once, if not twice.

Ben Waters of Digital Magnet
http://digital-magnet.uk

 *'Promo Power Supremacy' is easy to read and provides a step-by-step guide to using promotional products to market your business in the most successful way possible. Mo's conversational, honest style is refreshing. The key take away points at the end of each section help you to consolidate what you have just read, plan your strategy and take action.*

It's clear that Mo is passionate about helping his customers and he has really put an enormous amount of thought and effort into his book. The book goes beyond promotional products and can be applied to many aspects of your marketing strategy. The 'great little tips' are invaluable and, as you read the book, these gems click into place. I personally had lots of light bulb moments and will be implementing Mo's suggestions, tips and strategies as soon as possible.

If you own your own business or you are a marketing manager, this book is a must read.

Lorraine Windsor of The Social Matrix
http://www.socialmatrixhub.co.uk

WHAT PEOPLE ARE SAYING ABOUT WORKING WITH MO AND HIS TEAM

My Money Club is a money saving membership club, and we needed to send a pen within the welcome packs.

Club Row Creations, after a very brief call, supplied us with sample pens so we could choose ones that would be right for us.

We selected the pen, sent in the logo and that was it - so simple. The product is well-presented and excellent quality, and the service you get from the staff - Wills especially - is great. I can place an order at the last minute and they are delivered within days.

Kristian Benham of My Money Club
http://mymoneyclub.net

My problem was rewarding customer loyalty, and raising exposure.

Club Row Creations presented a range of items and offered me complimentary samples so that I could see the quality of the items for myself. Quality was a top priority to reflect my brand.

Club Row Creations remained engaged in a non-pushy way until I was ready to implement my vision.

During the creative stage, the dynamics were fantastic: proactive and patient, with some great design initiatives. They bent over backwards to accommodate my changing requests, but the whole process, from concept to formalising the order, was very quick, thanks to same day, back-and-forth communications.

Turnaround times for fulfilment were impressive too.

I am now the proud owner of water bottles featuring my logo, golf umbrellas, earphones and Swiss USB chargers. Last but not least, the pens! These are sleek, in line with my brand's colour (the Call to Action being my website address), and they work!

If you want a partnership with a supplier who is working alongside you, and will avoid you the embarrassment of cheap stuff that does your image no favours, I highly recommend Club Row Creations.

Ariana Torti of Le Massage of Mayfair

We are a small social media company and, like most businesses, we highly value our clients, continuously striving to give great customer service. We wanted to give our customers a high-quality gift to reflect how much we value them, but also something they could regularly use to keep us at the forefront of their minds.

We approached Club Row Creations, as we knew they would give us some great ideas. They came up with some suggestions but the one we fell in love with was a grey, Smart Power Tower bank branded with our company logo. This was perfect for our company as it's our job to give our customers a consistent social presence online

We were sent design ideas and a final proof, so we could see what the delivered items would look like. Nothing was too much trouble for the team at Club Row, including the short timescale we asked for. Wills went above and beyond to deliver on time.

The final result is nothing short of wow! We are so happy and so are our clients. Thanks Club Row!

Lorraine Windsor of The Social Matrix
www.socialmatrixhub.co.uk

 *For almost eight years, we have used conference boxes to contain all the paperwork, spare keys, etc., as part of the handover to customers when they collect their new motorcycles. This was something we'd been very happy with, that is, until we received your new catalogue.*

Basically, while the boxes looked professional and did the job, they weren't the easiest things to transport on a motorcycle. Then came the answer to this problem in glorious technicolour - a conference bag with a shoulder strap.

A quick email to Russell (as usual it was a last minute thing) and in no time we had quotes and a copy of our new art work in place ready for our final decision.

Decision made, another quick email to confirm the order and it was feet up, happy in the knowledge it was all in hand. Typically, the bags have arrived ahead of schedule and look fantastic. We love them and the customers love them - perfect!

Sharon Claridge of Bahnstormer
www.bahnstormer.co.uk

I wanted a welcome gift I could give to members of my Inner Circle group and Mo and his team really did come up with the goods.

I chose a mobile device charger called the Power Tower.

Mo sent me details, an image and prices straightaway (he also suggested some little velvet pouches to put them in, which I took him up on). When I confirmed my order, I immediately received confirmation and a layout. They kept me up-to-date with progress and even delivered a day early.

I'd never go anywhere else for my promotional items and highly recommend Club Row Creations. If you want great ideas, high-quality products and an easy, hassle free life, Mo's your man!

Stewart Gibson of GP Retail
www.gpretail.co.uk

I needed a little gift I could send out to my existing customers as a small thank you for all the business they've given us over the years.

I didn't want something they'd just look at and never use, I wanted something they'd actually think was useful, and I didn't have a clue what that would be. I also didn't have the will to try and look for something myself.

Mo and his team came up with this brilliant little USB charger – everyone has times when their mobile runs out of battery, especially these days with Facebook. They found the ideal little gift and handled all the aggro of sourcing and shipping. They got them engraved and shipped over to me, and they look great.

We've got long-term subscription customers who we're always talking to, so I wanted to send them something they'd find useful rather than some crappy little thing they'd throw in the bin. Mo and his team delivered – my customers love them. It was so easy and totally hassle free.

Steve Barnett of Hexagon IT
www.hexagoncloud.co.uk

I was stuck — I was running an expensive business event and I wanted to give the delegates something special as a 'welcome gift'. The only problem was... I'd left things to the last minute and didn't have more than a couple of days to get everything made up and delivered.

But Mo stepped up to the plate and whacked things right out of the park. Not only did he get everything done on time and deliver outstanding quality, but he delivered it personally, just to make sure I got it — T-shirts, caps, bags... the lot.

Now, that's what I call service.

Of course, service like this doesn't come with the lowest price tag. But, then, that's not what I want. What I want is things done right, done right the first time, and done without a whole load of hassle. That to me is worth paying extra for. And that's what I got.

Jon McCulloch
www.jonmcculloch.com

Every October, we hold an annual conference where we invite our existing and potential customers to learn about the latest topical news and ways of staying ahead of their competitors.

This year, we are revamping all of our promotional items and, as always, we wanted a gift that's a bit different and special to thank our customers for their business each year. So the challenge was on for Wills at Club Row. He was tasked with finding some modern funky mugs, quality pens and notebooks and bags to complement Mo's suggestion earlier this year of Powerlink cables.

I sent Wills a couple of pens that I had ordered over the years and specified which one I always get asked for. It seems such a simple item to buy, but the comments you get from colleagues can range from the pen feeling cheap or not writing as nicely as other pens, so it's important to get it right. On the other hand, the pens Wills sourced for me are constantly being asked for.

Then, we wanted a mug that was a bit different. The options Wills sent me certainly gave me food for thought. So I got a sample of the one I liked best before placing the order. Wills even gave me a few choices on the Powerlink cables, as these will be so useful for our customers.

Jacqui Smith of Computers Unlimited
http://3ddesign.unlimited.com

We do a lot of work with our local schools and attend fetes, fairs and community events throughout the year. The 8-14 year olds are a tough group to connect with, and promotional goods help us do the job: Frisbees, coasters, bugs, bands, USB sticks, clappers, pens, t-shirts, thunder sticks, water bottles, kit bags, sweatbands, and more.

Over the years, Club Row has advised, inspired, mentored and educated us on our choices.

We are a very busy marketing department and we often task Mo and his team with coming up with the goods (literally) and they never fail us – short turnarounds, great communication, dedication and first-class customer service always ensures a satisfactory outcome.

Sarah Buckle of New Forest Health and Leisure
www.newforest.gov.uk/healthandleisure

We needed to find a quality gift for our conference attendees and our biggest challenge was to find something we hadn't given out before, something our guests could use but also enjoy. It was a very important event as we were celebrating our 50-year anniversary.

Wills and Russell came to meet me and I was very impressed with the range of products they suggested, and especially with how well prepared for the meeting they were. I have to find a gift every year and this was the first time a company presented their services in such a professional and comprehensive way. I was blown away by their enthusiasm and 'can do' attitude!

We chose a very nice, high-quality Balmain Pen and some lovely goodie bags. The process of choosing the items, proofing the artwork and placing the order was simple, efficient and quick. The team followed up during production and kept me in the loop of how things were progressing. The items arrived well before the required date, which was very helpful.

Elvira Lautenschlager of Subway
www.subway.co.uk

 *I work for National Grid, but in my spare time I belong to a belly-dancing group.*

Recently, we planned a trip to Barcelona, incorporating a Flamenco workshop. Prior to our trip, I won a prize from one of Mo's competitions and thought it would be nice to use it with something useful and not too expensive that could advertise the group.

After many discussions with Russell, we settled on a big shopper bag that was just the right size to carry costumes and props. We talked about the colour, the message to be printed, and its design. I thought it was a good idea to put an image on the bag. So, I spent some time on the internet and found an image of a belly dancer's silhouette.

Russell then sent me the proof and it was perfect. No amendments were necessary. The overall effect was very classy and the girls were delighted with them. We proudly used them in Barcelona.

Irma Gregg of Sitara Dance
www.sitaradance.co.uk

CONTENTS

FOREWORD...**25**

INTRODUCTION..**29**

Why I've Written This Book...............................30

Who This Book is For.......................................30

How to Get the Best From This Book................31

Chapter 1: The 7 Reasons Why Most Promotional Products Fail Miserably and How to Fix That........**33**

Reason 1 – Failing to Understand the Importance of Quality..34

Reason 2 – The Wrong Type of Products.............39

Reason 3 – Choosing the Wrong Type of Decoration........40

Reason 4 – Not Knowing Who to Trust...............43

Reason 5 – Going it Alone...................................45

Reason 6 – Failing to Plan..................................48

Reason 7 – Being Unaware of the 3 Golden Rules............49

Golden Rule # 1 – The product you choose must ooze quality..49

Golden Rule # 2 – Ensure the product is useful............50

Golden Rule # 3 – Make it different.......................50

Chapter 2: How to Create Your Perfect Range.......**53**

Why There's No Quick Fix...................................53

Be different...54

The 6 Simple Steps to Creating Your Perfect Range 57

Step 1 – Decide the who, the what and the when *58*

Step 2 – Start hunting *60*

Step 3 - Brainstorming *63*

Step 4 - Make a phone call *64*

Step 5 - Gather samples *66*

Step 6 - Make your final selection *69*

**Chapter 3: The Seven Motives for Investing in
Promotional Products** **73**

The 7 Motives Explained 73

Motive #1 - To create awareness *73*

Motive # 2 - To attract the right audience *75*

Motive #3 - To help start a meaningful relationship *79*

Motive #4 - To get new business *81*

Motive # 5 - To get someone to buy from you – ethically . *83*

Motive #6 - To thank them for doing business with you .. *85*

Motive #7 - To get them to come back again and again ... *88*

Chapter 4: The Dream 100 Concept **91**

What is the Dream 100 Concept? 91

*The fastest way to build your business is to target
the best clients* *92*

The Dream 100 Strategy 95

Stage 1: Choose the companies you want to do business with 95

Stage 2: Choose your products and your Call to Action ..96

Stage 3: Create your Dream 100 campaign 98

Chapter 5: Promotional Products in Action 105

Real Life Examples of How Promotional Products Have Worked Incredibly Well 105

Promotional products in action #1 – Mo's lapsed customer campaign 106

Promotional products in action #2 – Jan's awareness campaign 113

Promotional products in action #3 – Mark's staff retention record 114

Promotional products in action #4 – Crispin's warm and fuzzy T-shirts 116

Promotional products in action #5 – Mo's Dream 100 campaign 117

Chapter 6: Marketing Campaigns and How to Make Them Effective 121

Initial Contact and Nurturing 121

Turning leads into paying customers 123

After sales campaigns 126

Keeping hold of your existing customers 128

Turning Your Customers into Raving Fans 135

Chapter 7: The Consequences of Staying Still 143

Things Can be Done Faster Than Ever Before....................143

Things Can be Done Now That Couldn't be Done
Before 144

The Service we Give Now Can be Better Than Ever
Before 145

The Past *145*

The Present..*146*

The AIDA Principle 147

The Future *151*

Promotional Products Will be Changing Faster
Than Ever Before..152

Everything that can be, will be automated *153*

Personalised webshops...*155*

No minimum webshops *156*

CONCLUSION 161

NEXT STEPS 167

ABOUT THE AUTHOR..169

ACKNOWLEDGEMENTS..170

RESOURCES 171

Dedication

To all the rubbish promotional products out there that are stuffed in people's drawers all around the country and never get a chance to do their job properly because they're so damn boring and of no real use to anyone.

FOREWORD

I was delighted to be asked by Mo to write his foreword. For the past nine years, I've headed up the British Promotional Merchandise Association and, as one of our most active members, Mo is as passionate as I am about promotional branded products and the effect they have in the marketing mix. Prior to joining the bpma, I ran my own rewards and incentive agency in Cambridgeshire, and I have also purchased and used promotional products all my life.

The UK promotional merchandise industry is worth around £1bn, but it's still a very small percentage of total marketing spend. For me, it represents one of the biggest opportunities for brands to engage with their clients, especially when you consider how much money is spent on printed collateral such as catalogues and flyers, when much of these are thrown away. But an effective promotional product that's useful and relevant is kept for an average of 2.5 years. I still have products I received over 20 years ago. The bpma has invested in research extensively over the last decade. We discovered that successful promotional product should be:

- High quality (product and branding)
- Memorable
- Relevant to the target audience
- Useful
- Long-lasting

We also found out that if they had larger budgets, marketers would spend a lot more on promotional merchandise, suggesting they see the value of them. There are so many different uses for a promotional product, such as:

- Advertising & Marketing - for campaigns.

- Sales Promotion – self-liquidating (where the consumer pays a low price for a premium but has to collect tokens or proofs of purchase).

- Awards & Rewards – long service and presentation plaques for achievement.

- Brand Awareness & Rebranding – one of the most popular ways in which merchandise is used.

- Cause Awareness – many charities and pressure groups use branded clothing, for example, as a powerful way to convey a message.

- Club & School Identification – branded uniform and badges.

- Conferences & Events – merchandise works well in conveying a theme for an event and a takeaway.

- Direct Mail - this has proven to have a greater response rate with a branded gift.

- Health & Safety Recycling Schemes – to create a powerful educational message.

- New Branch Openings – typically branded T-shirts and balloons would be covered here.

- Souvenirs – this is a huge sector and a spinoff from promotional merchandise, as in most cases they are purchased.

Merchandise has an overwhelming impact and impression ratio. For example, the average person drinks around 1500 cups of tea and coffee a year, so the value of creating a constant reminder to a recipient in the form of a mug is very effective. Equally, think about the amount of times it rains a year (on average around 147). A branded umbrella has the opportunity to be used many times throughout the year. The other thing I always talk about is 'conversational merchandise', in other words, something that a recipient receives that's either very relevant, super cool, and/or very useful, so much so that they want to talk about it to their friends, colleagues or family, and/or share it online via social media. This all adds to the amount of media impressions that brand receives. An example of this would be a wooden whistle I picked up at Internet World over 15 years ago. The software company, Commission Junction, used the strapline "Sales arriving daily" and the whistle makes the noise of a stream train. I have shown this now to over 5,000 people. Everyone at the exhibition wanted one of these products.

Bags and pens are still the most popular products, but there has been a considerable rise in electronic items. That's no surprise given the reliance we have on computers and phones.

Buyers also face the challenge of constantly finding new and exciting ideas. My answer to this is often driven by the message you put on the product, and a useful and relevant product with a cool strapline can be extremely effective. Some products even have multiple uses. For example, a bottle opener/penknife for a key ring, or a pen that has a stylus pen on the other end of it.

So, when you are considering using promotional products, really think about your target audience and what their needs might be. You will get far better engagement if you do this. Sometimes, it's better to ask your promotional advisor to come up with ideas that best meet your brief. They can then search the market so you don't have to, or even have it made to order.

Happy promoting...

Gordon Glenister

Director General

British Promotional Merchandise Association

INTRODUCTION

Congratulations! You've taken the first step to becoming an expert in using promotional products in a way that will get you noticed (without wasting money) and drive your business forward.

Everything I share with you in this book is absolutely true, and it works. How do I know? Because I've personally tried and tested most of the strategies and tactics that sit between the covers of this book. You'll even see actual results and real life examples from people who've achieved great success because of the clever way they've used promotional products in their marketing campaigns.

Having said that, here's the thing...

Everything we start, unless we follow through to completion, ends up in the *Good Idea Graveyard*. You know, that sad place where all those good ideas you know will work suddenly get lost and forgotten about. I really don't want the ideas that'll undoubtedly flash through your mind as you start reading this book - those light bulb moments of sudden inspiration, realisation and enlightenment - to become lost.

So I want to prepare you...

All the successful tactics and strategies you'll come across in this book won't work for you if you just read about them. Neither will they work unless you're prepared to roll up your sleeves and get to work. It's like everything you do in life, if you want success you need to put all your effort into achieving it.

Here's the good news...

When you begin reading, the things you'll learn will start to become obvious. Ideas will quickly form in your mind, but like everything that's new, you're likely to feel uneasy about getting started. That's fine, because I've written this book in a way that'll help you out and make implementation that much easier.

Why I've Written This Book

There's a lot of nonsense talk about promotional products and how you need them to promote your brand.

I'm sorry to disappoint you, and I'll probably make other suppliers spit blood for saying this, but people in this industry who endorse the myth that you need to buy promotional products to create brand awareness are talking total B.S.

As you'll discover, people don't actually care about your brand and, unless you're a huge corporate with millions to spend on it, you really will be wasting your money.

So the reason I've written this book is to set the record straight by sharing everything I've learnt (the hard way) over the last 29 years. I want your investment in promotional products to have the best chance of giving *you* a good return on investment. Implementing just one of the many strategies you'll come across in this book will make a huge difference to the success you'll have.

Who This Book is For

This book is primarily aimed at helping anyone who is involved in marketing full-time. Be that organising events, seminars or trade shows. It's also valuable to anyone who owns their own business and wants to attract more of the right kind of customers (rather than the ones you dread dealing with).

If you're just starting out, or are new to promotional products, then this book will give you all the information you'll need to become an expert. It'll help you to keep your name in front of your customers and prospects, so they will be more likely to choose you rather than one of your competitors the next time they're looking for the products or services you offer.

How to Get the Best From This Book

While each chapter I've written tells a different story, it's important to read it in sequential order. It'll help you understand how to avoid the pitfalls and mistakes most people make when investing in promotional products. I've written it in such a way that the information in the subsequent chapters will be simpler to grasp once you understand the principles behind them. Then you'll understand just how powerful the strategies and tactics are, and how easy they are to implement.

As you read each chapter and ideas begin to develop, take notes, highlight pages and re-read before you implement. At the end of each chapter, I've highlighted the key points to help you with the important facts you need to remember.

The hardest and most difficult thing to do is to start - everything else is just momentum. Once you begin, it'll surprise you how easy it will all suddenly become. So read, learn and, most important of all... implement!

CHAPTER 1

The 7 Reasons Why Most Promotional Products Fail Miserably and How to Fix That

Ok, before we dive in let's just look at why promotional items fail so miserably.

Over the years, I've observed how some people choose their promotional items, and I just don't understand why anybody would invest money without getting the best out of it.

Sometimes, it's left to the very last minute and that's understandable. If you're organising an event or have some sort of promotion going on, there's so much else to worry about: invites, booking the venue, sorting out the room and lots of other stuff, so promotional items are usually last on the list.

Sometimes, people just decide they want some pens with their name on them, without really thinking about what they're going to do with them or what benefit they'll get from them.

In truth, most promotional items don't work. They don't succeed in doing what they should be doing, and that is making your company money.

So, if they're not making your company money, what's the point?

To be honest, I'm not happy (and neither is my team) just taking someone's money if they're not going to benefit.

It's not because we're nice people – it's actually in our own self-interest. If you're making money from stuff we supply to you, you'll come back again and again and, hopefully, tell other people about us too.

I'll go on to explain the reasons why most promotional products fail and give tips to help you make yours a success. Hopefully, when you've got to Reason 7, you'll be able to choose your promotional products better, quicker, easier and with less hassle. So, let's get started.

Reason 1 – Failing to Understand the Importance of Quality

Why spend money on promotional products?

Now that's actually a very good question and there's a very simple answer.

It makes YOU money, but only if it's done the right way (I'll cover that in a bit).

Before I do, here are some important and interesting facts about promotional items:

- UK businesses spend over £900 million a year on promotional products – that's almost £1 billion.

- Promotional merchandise can deliver a higher, or at least the same, ROI as TV, radio, online and print advertising.

This means you don't have to spend the large sums of money that TV and radio demand to achieve a good return on investment. And, unlike online and print advertising, your name and message will stay with them a lot longer.

- 66% of business people interviewed said they could remember the brand on the promotional product they received during the last year – so your company name and message will stay in the minds of the people you most want to do business with.

- When asked if they would be more likely to do business with a company after receiving a promotional item, a massive 79% of the 14,728 people interviewed confirmed they would be.

When you invest your hard-earned cash or your limited budget on promotional merchandise, you need to be crystal clear why you're doing it and what you expect in return.

There are five basic reasons for using promotional merchandise, which are:

1. A Form of Advertising – To make people aware of you, your products and your services.

A big mistake a lot of people make when investing in low cost promotional items is to order, say, a few thousand cheap pens with their logo printed on them, and then hand them out willy-nilly.

Big mistake. Why? Because so many other people are doing this, and your cheap pens will just get put with all the other cheap pens and forgotten about.

Now, I'm not saying promotional pens or low cost promotional products are a total waste of time. They do have their place and handing them out at, say, a seminar or conference can help people to remember you, as long as they're useful, a bit different and don't look cheap.

I'll actually come back to this in a bit and show you an example of how you can have a promotional product that is great quality, stands out and, most importantly, doesn't actually cost you any more money.

2. Thank You Gifts – To thank someone for doing business with you.

Don't underestimate how powerful thank you gifts are.

It tells your customer you really value their business and it makes them feel important too... which they are. It also shows a caring side and it's a great way to keep the relationship going after the sale. And, this is a biggie...

...the Law of Reciprocity kicks in: *"If I give you something, you'll want to give me something in return."*

I've never actually understood why we get a tumbleweed moment from a supplier the minute our orders have been delivered.

3. Incentives – To motivate someone to do something.

An example of this is to get people to spend more with you. Something like: *"Spend £100 and get this amazing Power Bank mobile device charger worth £15."* Or, how about: *"Sign up for my workshop by the 31st and I'll give you a set of earphones absolutely free"?*

4. To Acknowledge Membership of a Group or Company – To get people feeling part of a team.

People want to belong to a family, to a sports team or to a work group, and branding products with your company logo and message helps people to feel that belonging.

The next time you visit an Apple store you'll see everyone wearing with pride a blue or red T-shirt with the white Apple logo emblazoned on the front.

This is also a big thing for one of our customers based in Mountain View, California. Whenever they have training, everyone gets kitted out with a T-shirt, hoody, baseball cap, lanyard, pen and bag.

5. To Sell – *Makes you money and gets other people promoting your business.*

This is a really big thing for big brands and charities where people want to buy something to support the cause.

A company that does this brilliantly is Guinness. They have literally anything you can imagine for sale with their logo on it, from luxury truffles and gourmet crisps to Christmas baubles and even fluffy slippers.

Ok, so here's my really good example of how you can make your advertising product stand out from the crowd.

On the next page you will see a selection of promotional pens, they'll cost you around the 30p – 40p mark.

Now compare them with the next image. They have a soft rubberised finish, they are triangular in shape and they ooze style, sophistication and originality.

I'm gonna show off a bit now...

Its floating-ball-jumbo refill means a smoother and more graceful writing experience in comparison to conventional refills, and it'll last three times longer than the cheaper ones... three kilometres of writing compared to one kilometre.

Figure 1: Typical selection of promotional pens

Compare the image above, to the little beauties below.

Figure 2: Triangular in shape

So, at around £1 each, it won't actually cost you anymore than the cheaper pens, when you consider the lifetime value.

Wills, one of the team, is still using the triangular pen I gave him two years ago, though it does have a new refill and a different barrel and clip. And I think the push button is different too. But hey...

You'll get the chance to grab yourself a free sample later in the book, so keep reading.

Reason 2 – The Wrong Type of Products

Now, you'd probably think this is all just common sense stuff. You consider the business you're in, the customers you want to attract, you have a hunt around and – hey presto! – YOU have the perfect range of products.

Wrong. Why? I'll tell you in a bit.

But before I do, here are a few interesting facts and figures from a survey involving buyers of promotional products:

- When asked how vital it is to purchase a promotional product that is **appropriate** to their intended audience, 79% of people said either important or very important.

- 76% said their perception of how their audience will **respond** to the item was either important or very important - get it wrong and your name will stick in people's minds for the wrong reasons.

So, going back to what I said earlier... it's not always as simple as just having a quick look and finding the perfect promotional products, there's other stuff you need to think about too.

Things like...

"What if my customers don't appreciate them?"

"What if the quality of the product when it's delivered is awful?"

"Is investing in this product a good use of my budget?"

"Will my supplier deliver on time?"

Some of these points we'll be covering later, but for now, here are three little tips to get us started:

1. **Be consistent** - Make sure your branded products are consistent with your organisation's reputation – Remember: the products you choose will be a reflection of your company in the eyes of others. Buy cheap and boring and that's how people will remember you.

2. **Get a reaction** - Your choice of products should be more influenced by how your audience will respond – In other words, buy promotional products that'll get a reaction. Something different will stick in people's minds and be a talking point in the office, so don't be afraid to be different.

3. **Pick stuff you would love to receive yourself** – When you're choosing promotional products (this is probably a bit of a strange thing to say), pick stuff you would love to own. People tend to buy from people similar to themselves.

Reason 3 – Choosing the Wrong Type of Decoration

Ever wondered why embroidered letters can sometimes look a bit spidery and illegible? Well, I'll show you how to fix that in a bit.

What I'll do at the end of this reason is show you how cool a well thought through decorated product can look.

Ok, so first of all, the one big thing your customers and prospects really don't care about...

...your logo.

It's absolutely true. Unless you're a well-known brand like Google, Apple, Disney or Coca-Cola, no one really cares about your logo. Apart from maybe your partner (because they want you to be happy) and, possibly, your bank manager (because he wants your money).

All people are really interested in is what you can do for them... so don't make your logo the main feature of your branding.

Other than your logo, and I'd suggest you make this as small as possible, there are three things you need to consider adding to your promotional products.

1. **Your website address.** People can look you up when they need to.

2. **Your message, or a strap line of some sort**. Then people will know what you do and how you can help them. For example, *"The world's favourite airline"* or *"Probably the best beer in the world."*

3. **An appropriate Call to Action.** We recently sent out boomerangs to lapsed customers basically telling them, *"Just like a boomerang, we want you to come back to us."* The Call to Action was asking them to go to a webpage and claim a £50 voucher (I'll share the results of this campaign in Chapter 5).

Now, when it comes to decoration, sometimes it's best to ask the experts. They know their products and what works best. Some metal pens, for example, look beautiful when engraved, but printing them could result in your company details slowly disappearing over time as the ink starts to come away (it's also not a bad idea to ask how permanent the decoration method is and what sort of guarantee is in place before you order).

There are so many methods of decoration these days. For clothing alone, there are six different methods of printing. The one you select is dependent on how you want the design to look, how you'd like it displayed, the type of fabric the garment's made from and the quantity you require.

GREAT LITTLE TIP

When you're having garments embroidered, ensure any lettering is at least 4mm tall and, if it's a fleece or towel, ask your supplier to add backing stitches to prevent your design from sinking into the pile of the fabric.

Ok, so now it's *'how cool a well thought through decorated product can look'* time.

This is what we do to thank our new customers. (See image on page 43.)

We send them a little cube in the post, gift wrapped with their name and a *"thank you for your recent order"*. *"Thank you"* is repeated in lots of different languages.

Figure 3: Gift wrapped mug

Inside is a black mug which is made from smoked glass with a subtle self colour design. Cool or what?

Figure 4: Really cool decorated product

Reason 4 – Not Knowing Who to Trust

I'll show you why this is in just three simple steps.

Before I start though, I'd like to point out that most

43

promotional product suppliers are very good at what they do, and it's not my intention to rubbish my competitors or accuse anyone of any wrong doing, dishonesty or lack of professionalism.

Besides, anyone who does offer a bad service won't stay in business for very long anyway.

The reason for me sharing my knowledge with you today is to help you spot those suppliers who maybe haven't been doing the job for very long and just don't understand promotional products as well as the experts. Perhaps they use printing companies, decorators and factories that are not the best around. Trust me, there are a few.

We actually 'black list' companies that mess up more than twice, for doing things like: Not telling us about a problem until it's too late, having an issue with quality they can't fix and constantly failing to respond to calls and emails.

So, let's get started.

Now, rather than telling you what to avoid, I'll show you what you can do to at least reduce the headaches, lessen the problems and avoid companies that seem to make processes complicated, hard work and, sometimes, just downright painful.

And let's be honest, we've all experienced them, both at work and in our personal lives.

Here are three very simple and probably obvious things, but, if you follow them, you won't go far wrong.

When looking for a supplier:

1. **Ask a colleague or friend if they can recommend someone.** This is dead easy and it takes a lot of the risk away.

Although you may not actually know the supplier yourself, they come highly recommended and the chances are you'll receive the same outstanding service your friend did.

2. **Make sure they have some sort of guarantee.** If a supplier has an impressive guarantee, it tells you two things about them.

One – they are more focused on making sure you get exactly what you want, when you want it.

Two – if something does go wrong at least you know there will be none of those, *"yeah but, no but"* moments.

The guarantee should be something like: *"If you are not completely satisfied, for any reason whatsoever, we will replace your order as fast as we possibly can free of charge."* This means they're probably a safe bet.

3. **Check for testimonials** – see what other people are saying about the supplier.

It's all very well for them to tell you how good they are... they're not gonna say they're rubbish, are they?

If someone else is telling you that, it makes it all the more believable. The easiest way to do this is to check their website and impartial sites such as Google reviews. Also ask them for the name of someone they've done business with that you can call or email.

Reason 5 – Going it Alone

Imagine this: you're a small business owner or you work for a company in the marketing or events department.

Chances are you don't have the luxury of spending all your time just buying promotional products. There's lots of other stuff you need to look after – organising exhibitions, sorting out press releases, booking venues, sending out invites and probably a handful of other activities.

Now, imagine being able to pick up the phone, speak to someone about an upcoming event, product launch or whatever it is you need products for and, rather than *you* having to spend lots of time hunting for promotional products that are relevant for the occasion and different enough to create the interest you want them to, it's all done for you.

Promotional Product Specialists are experts in all things related to promotional items.

- They have access to extensive databases that contain literally hundreds of thousands of promotional products.

- They are in tune with the latest trends, including hot items and the newest best-selling products.

- The other huge advantage in using a promotional specialist on a regular basis is that you build up that all-important relationship, and they get to understand the stuff that works best for you.

Here's a really good example of how well this works...

A good customer of mine calls me up looking for quality products for a designer brand. All the products need to reflect the high-quality of the brand and the colour theme of black and gold.

Here are just two of around a dozen items we uncovered:

Figure 5: Pen with style

Pens - black with gold nose cone.

Interestingly, this was not a standard option and it was only because we asked that we discovered the manufacturer had a few thousand gold cones left over from a previous order.

And how about these beauties – actual gold plated business card holders. They went down a storm.

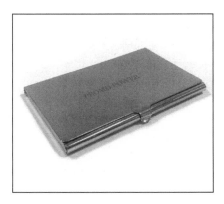

Figure 6: Gold plated card holder

> *So, just like most things you do...leave it to the experts.*

When your car's not working, what would you rather do? Tinker around with it yourself or get yourself a good mechanic?

Reason 6 – Failing to Plan

Ok, so this tip is boring – but it can save you so much time and avoid a lot of hassle.

Although it's probably the un-sexiest and least fun bit when it comes to investing in promotional products, getting the planning right will save you numerous headaches.

The trick is to plan early and avoid leaving everything to the last minute.

A big problem is that whenever you're organising an event or an activity that requires promotional products, it's very easy to leave them until last and then you end up limiting yourself regarding what you can have.

So, what you can do to help avoid this is:

- Forewarn your promotional product expert that something's coming up in a couple of months' time, and get them to start the ball rolling.

- Make sure you order everything to arrive ideally two weeks, but at least a full week, before the big day. This means that if anything does go wrong, you'll be aware of the problem in time and be able to take corrective action.

- Choose suppliers you can trust... don't buy on price alone but rather buy from someone who you know will look after you.

- When you place your order and send in your artwork, make sure the supplier confirms acceptance of your order, receipt of your artwork and that they can meet your deadline – it's so easy to email everything over and then three days later discover they didn't receive it.

- Call your supplier two days before the dispatch date to make sure everything is going according to plan. This will give you peace of mind that your order will be on time.

The thing is, most good suppliers won't need chasing because they're on top of everything and will save you all this, but it won't do any harm to have a few reminders in place.

Reason 7 – Being Unaware of the 3 Golden Rules

Having a simple tick box system regarding this when you're choosing your promotional products will help.

Now, my golden rules are probably going to be really obvious to you when I walk you through them, but... you'd be surprised how easy it is to forget the three things that make a promotional item highly prized, loved and treasured.

Golden Rule # 1 – The product you choose must ooze quality

91% of people interviewed in a survey about promotional products said the **quality** of the item was either important or extremely important. That's almost every single person asked.

Now, choosing high-quality products doesn't mean you have to spend a fortune on them. Simply avoid the cheap, nasty stuff. Believe me, there's a lot out there. A simple bit of advice would be to spend as much as you can afford rather than as little as you can get away with. Remember: the promotional items you give out say a lot about you and your company.

Golden Rule # 2 – Ensure the product is useful

In the same survey, when asked about the **usefulness** of the item, a staggering 93% said it was either very or extremely important.

It's the usefulness of the item - not its perceived cost - that will determine how long recipients keep it.

Golden Rule # 3 – Make it different

Avoid **boring**. If the product is different to most similar items it will get noticed, and it's more likely to be a talking point in the office or between a group of people.

Here are a couple of products you definitely won't see every day...

Figure 7: Quality mints

A tin of mints... but the mints are gold (these were another product that went with the black and gold pens I showed you earlier).

Figure 8: Useful and different

And how about, for the launch of a new fragrance with an outdoor woodland theme, camo toilet paper?

So, remember the Three Golden Rules:
QUALITY – USEFUL – DIFFERENT

KEY TAKE AWAY POINTS ARE:

- ✔ **When investing in promotional products** – Be clear with what you want them to do for you and what you expect in return.

- ✔ **Don't sacrifice quality** – Spend as much as you can afford rather than as little as you can get away with.

- ✔ **When choosing your promotional products** – Make sure they are in tune with your organisation's reputation.

- ✔ **Remember the golden rules** – Quality, useful, different.

CHAPTER 2

How to Create Your Perfect Range

Why There's No Quick Fix

As you discovered earlier, choosing a promotional product that does exactly what you want it to do isn't always as easy as you might think.

So, choosing a whole range of products that complement each other, have the wow factor so your target audience remembers your name for all the right reasons, and follows the 3 Golden Rules (quality, useful, different) can be a challenge, but not that difficult, as you'll discover in this chapter.

I always say, *"If you're going to do something, do it the best you can."* Spending just a few hours choosing promotional products is not going to create that perfect range. The products won't be as effective as they could be, and you won't be making the best use of your money. Putting in that little bit of extra effort will make a huge difference.

As a small aside, I'll never forget something said by Barry

Shamus at a business summit I attended a few years back. He was talking about how good customer service is the absolute minimum requirement in business (who would do business with someone and expect anything less than good customer service?).

Anyway, he said something along the lines of, *"Forget about going the extra mile, all you need to do is go the extra inch."*

When you think about it, he's absolutely right. The garage that cleans your car after repairing it is a small thing, but it makes a huge difference. The restaurant that gives you a free bottle of wine to take home with you after you've had your meal costs them very little but will get you talking to your friends about them.

My point here is that putting in a small amount of extra effort will give you big rewards.

Be different

The one big thing about many of your competitors is that they don't have a clue when it comes to promotional products. They simply look at what others are doing and follow them.

Here's the thing: when you think about it, 85% of businesses in the UK go bust within the first five years of trading. That's huge, so I'll spell it out another way:

Almost every business in the UK fails within five years of starting up.

Probably one of the reasons for this is because they look at what their competitors are doing, assume it must be right, and copy them. Big mistake. The American author and speaker Earl Nightingale once said: *"Watch what everyone else does - do the opposite. The majority is always wrong."*

Of course, he didn't mean that literally, but his big point is this: **Be different.**

Think about it: if you do things the same as your competitors, and this also applies to your promotional products, why would anyone choose you? There's only one reason why and that's because you're the cheapest and, let's face it, no one is ever the cheapest. There's always someone out there so desperate for business they'll take the job on at any cost. I've known companies that have gone out at a loss in the hope they'll make money on the next order. Trouble is, once you've done it the first time, you'll do it again and again and, eventually, you'll end up becoming one of the 85%.

A great example of a company that does things differently is Apple, and it's no coincidence that it is the biggest company in the world.

An email I sent to my list a while back pretty much sums up how doing things differently to your competitors, which includes offering amazing customer service, wins every time.

Here it is...

Apple fixes bad backs too

It's true. Not only does Apple give brilliant service and great quality products it also helps cure back pain.

Let me explain and, at the same time, show you an example of brilliant service verses pretty poor service.

Because I'm away from time to time and need to be able to communicate with my friend, Mandy, I managed to persuade her to buy an iPad Mini so we can chat on Skype and FaceTime.

Now, usually when Mandy buys, she'll go with whatever does the job, as she can't always justify why she should spend more for something that does pretty much the same as something that costs less.

We went to a well-known electrical products and computer retailer and asked a sales guy standing at the front of the store how to go about buying an iPad Mini. *"You need to find someone who's free, I'm not allowed to leave this spot,"* he said misguidedly. (I would be surprised if he was told, *"Under no circumstances must you try and sell something to someone who has told you they want to buy something."*)

So, we waited and wandered around a bit before finally giving up. We decided, and I don't know why we didn't do this in the first place, to go to the Apple store... and what a difference.

As soon as we walked in and explained what we wanted, we were directed to a spot at the back of the store. An Apple guy who saw us sensed we wanted help, and although he was busy, he took the trouble to find someone to help us straightaway.

We were then witness to a 30-minute masterclass on *'How to make someone so impressed with quality and service, you simply cannot leave without buying.'* And the funny thing is, he wasn't trying to sell.

He explained a few things about the iPad Mini and the option of having it with or without retina display and then, when Mandy made her choice, he asked if she'd like help setting everything up so she could use her gadget straightaway.

In less than 30 minutes, not only was Mandy the proud owner of an iPad Mini with retina display (yup, she went for the more expensive option), it was all set up and she even knew how to use it.

So, you may be wondering, how does Apple fix back pain?

Well, a week or so earlier, Mandy pulled her back, big time, and she was still in pain earlier in the day.

We were sitting in a bar a few minutes after leaving the Apple store, Mandy playing with her new iPad Mini, huge grin on her face, and the expression of a child playing with her main present on Christmas day, and I asked her, *"Mands, how's the pain in your back now?"* Mandy replied something along the lines of: *"Pain? What pain? It's gone."*

Coincidence? Or could it be one of the strange things that happens to your body when you experience great joy and pleasure?

There's a great little exercise you can do to help you stand out from the crowd, which I'll share with you at the end of this chapter.

The 6 Simple Steps to Creating Your Perfect Range

It's actually not that difficult to put together your perfect promotional products range, as long as you're prepared to put in the effort and follow the simple 6-step process.

Ok, so let's get started.

Step I – Decide the who, the what and the when

The three things you need to establish before you even start thinking about promotional products are:

1. The Who – Who is your target audience?

Without being clear about the type of person you want to attract, you'll struggle to find products that'll engage them. There's little point in choosing a screwdriver set with six assorted screwdriver bits, an LED torch and a belt clip if you're targeting cosmetics companies (sounds unlikely? You'd be surprised).

If you think your target audience is anyone with a credit card, you really do need help. Why would you do business with an axe murderer who's just chopped someone up and stolen their credit card? (I'm sure you get my drift.)

If your client base is varied in terms of business types, create an avatar of your ideal customer and target that person. It's actually great fun to do and the more specific you make that person, the easier it is to engage with them.

An example could include stuff like:

- Man or woman, aged around 30 – 55 years old

- Works in a marketing-related job, for a company whose turn-over is £1million plus, and can also work for a large corporate

- Leads a healthy life, goes to the gym or does some sort of physical exercise a few times a week

- Loves food and eats healthily

- Travels a lot

This gives you an idea of the sort of promotional items that would appeal to them. It could be sports related, such as a gym bag, a miniature bottle of wine personalised with their name on the label, or a device charger they can keep with them while they're travelling.

It also goes without saying that your choice of promotional items should reflect the type of company you are and be in harmony with your products or services.

2. The What – What are they being used for?

If you use promotional products for lots of different purposes, or for different types of events, a good idea is to create a spreadsheet listing them all.

Events Schedule for 2016 / 2017

Name of Event	Type of Event	Date of Event
B2B Marketing Expo	Trade Show	15th Feb 2016
Dream 100 Campaign	Marketing Campaign	4th August 2016
Event Organisers Summit	Trade Show	10th Oct 2016
Coaching and Curry Day	Open Day	17th Nov 2016
B2B Marketing Expo	Trade Show	16th May 2017

Product Ideas	Power banks	Pens
B2B Marketing Expo	Y	N
Dream 100 Campaign	Y	N
Event Organisers Summit	Y	N
Coaching and Curry Day	Y	Y
B2B Marketing Expo	Y	N

Figure 9: Image of a spreadsheet

If it's a thank you gift for your top customers or a welcome gift for your new high spenders, it's obvious the item needs to be of more value than, for example, a lead generation item to attract more business.

You'll then have a clearer idea when you're searching what items fit where, and you'll also find that some items will fit perfectly into one or more event or purpose. It'll also help you to discard some items very quickly.

You can download your own template ready to use by visiting www.promopowersupremacy.co.uk

3. The When – When are they needed?

Another great time saver, and a huge benefit, is to add the dates your products are needed by in your spreadsheet, and also when you need to start looking and place your orders by (you'll find out why later in this chapter).

Although most promotional products can be turned around in just a few weeks, some of the more bespoke items will need a bit of sampling and development time, and could take as long as 10 – 12 weeks. So, getting the ball rolling sooner rather than later means you'll have far more options to consider.

Step 2 – Start hunting

Ok, so you now have your list of events and activities, you know exactly the type of person or company they need to appeal to, and you know the dates you need your promotional products by and the latest date you can get away with ordering them.

You should also ask yourself three other questions before you start hunting:

1. **What types of promotional products have I used before that worked well?**

2. **What shall I exclude?**

3. **What price ranges should they fit into?** It could be

as simple as low: under £2, mid: £2 - £5 and top of the range: £5 plus.

The hunting part is exactly that, the activity of searching for something. You're on the lookout for stuff that's new and different, so don't worry about basic stuff at this stage. Even if you already have in mind some products you may want to use, keep an open mind, you may find something that works better.

Create an ideas folder on your computer so you can keep all your images together. Then, start off by looking for products in the categories you know you need. It could be bags, notebooks, techie stuff or sweets. Whatever it is, focus on one product at a time. The trick here is to find stuff that follows the 3 golden rules – quality, useful, different – so keep them in the back of your mind.

GREAT LITTLE TIP

Brochures are a good starting place. Although some people prefer to look online these days, there are two big advantages to flicking through the pages of a brochure. One, it's a lot quicker scanning pages that contain up to a dozen items complete with the information you need than having to click on images to get more info. And two, it's sometimes easier on the eye and more fun to sit with a colleague flicking through pages.

So, when you receive brochures through the post, even if they're from someone you don't know or have no intention of dealing with, do think twice before you throw them in the bin, you could be chucking away a goldmine of ideas.

When you come across products you like the look of, even if they're from a supplier you don't know, go onto their website and see if they feature there (most promotional product brochures and catalogues these days are generic and produced by *'catalogue groups'* with a bespoke cover, so you may not see the same stuff on a supplier's website). In these cases, simply take a quick photo of the product and save it in your ideas folder.

Once you've exhausted all the brochure options, you can start looking online.

I have to be honest here, this is not an easy task and you do need to spend a fair amount of time looking if you want to find stuff that really is different. In most cases, even typing the words *"quality"*, *"useful"* or *"different"* before the product type you're looking for will bring up the same basic stuff. But perseverance and determination will bring you rewards.

It's important to remember you are just looking for ideas at this stage, so just blitz it. Simply copy the images of anything you see that are even remotely interesting and save them in your ideas folder. You can go through them later and get rid of anything you have second thoughts about.

You need to keep going until you've chosen between 50 – 100 products. The more you have the better. This process is likely to take up to 16 hours. If you spend less time, it's unlikely you'll find those hidden gems that tick all the boxes.

GREAT LITTLE TIP

Do your hunting in short periods of around two to four hours. Any longer and you'll become *'snow blind'* (everything starts to look the same and you'll find it impossible to differentiate between what's cool and relevant and what sucks). You'll also start to lose the will to live – trust me, I've been there many times.

Step 3 - Brainstorming

Now you have your huge selection of quality products, which are also useful and different, it's time to move onto the brainstorming phase.

Grab hold of a couple of colleagues (no more than two, otherwise there will be too many conflicting opinions), explain what the products are for and ask them to choose the most innovative ones – the ones that really have the "wow" factor.

Also, ask if there's anything they can think of that you may have missed. This tends to work incredibly well and you'll find that completely new related products are suddenly in the mix.

When you're making your final selection, add them to your spreadsheet in the columns for the different purposes and events. This is a brilliant use of your time because you'll now have ideas not just for the event you're planning, but other events later in the year. You'll also find that some products will cross over into more than one event.

GREAT LITTLE TIP

When you're making your final selection, be ruthless — *"if in doubt, throw it out,"* as my buying controller used to say during my fashion buyer days.

Step 4 - Make a phone call

You should now have your range of ideas, and here's where a bit of expert help and advice is needed.

Call up your Promotional Product Specialist, ask them to come and see you or do a Skype session where you can share screens. Show them the products you've selected and the events they're for. The more information you give them, the easier it'll be for them to help you.

Let them come up with either the products you've chosen, something similar or even a better alternative. If they're worth their salt, they'll also be able to suggest products you didn't even know existed.

Here's the thing: most Promotional Product Specialists have access to tens of thousands (10,000+) of product ideas. They use databases to select products by industry type, event type, price point, colour and delivery time. They are also kept up-to-date with all the latest trends and new products.

Here's what one of our customers said when we went to town on her product range:

"Dear Russell,

Just a really quick note to say thank you so much for the amazing meeting that we had yesterday.

You clearly put so much thought into your catalogue ideas and have really blown me away with the diligence and creativity that you have shown in coming up with ideas for our business. Also, the quality of the items that you showed me yesterday was truly outstanding.

I have so many ideas in the pipeline and will be working to pull together a cohesive plan.

But I wanted to thank you so much - your generosity of spirit, time and creativity are truly first rate. I look forward to working with you in the future to get some really amazing products together for our clients.

Mo – Russell Rocks!! And I loved your email today too.

Wishing you an amazing Christmas, if I don't speak to you before.

Best Regards,

Yinka"

To be honest, we did the whole thing for Yinka from start to finish, which probably explains why she was so blown away, she really didn't have a clue what to expect.

Excited about what I've said and want to know how we do it?

Have a look on the website below and all will be revealed...*www.promopowersupremacy.co.uk*

GREAT LITTLE TIP

Give your supplier as much time as you can to get back to you. For them to do a good job for you, they're likely to need a good two weeks or so.

The more time you allow them, the better the final range is likely to be.

Step 5 - Gather samples

Ok, so now you've done all the work, you can relax a little and get on with whatever else you need to do to make your event the best it can be.

When you finally receive your ideas catalogue from your supplier, go through it carefully, choose the products you want to know more about and ask them to send samples. Most suppliers won't charge you and it's crucial you see, feel and test everything before you place your final orders.

Here's a story I wrote about price not being the most important factor when you buy, which also perfectly illustrates why not seeing samples before you buy can result in disastrous consequences.

Price is so important

Two things happened over the last two days that proved to me just how important it is to pay the right price for stuff.

Pay the right price 1

Towards the end of last year, a good customer of ours asked about 2D and 3D memory sticks. They were to be totally bespoke and they wanted quite a large quantity.

We did all the usual stuff, including sending him details and prices. He made a few changes so there followed more details and more prices until finally we found exactly what he was looking for.

He decided to go for 3D memory sticks and asked us if we could match a very low price he'd been quoted by one of our competitors.

Now, we're not into doing things on the cheap just to get the order, because ultimately you get what you pay for, so we kindly turned down the offer of a great order and wished him well.

Anyway, our used-to-be good customer's 3D memory sticks arrived, but he wasn't a happy bunny because... they were 2D.

Figure 10: 2D and 3D Memory Sticks

Pay the right price 2

Again, just before Christmas, we helped Graham, a friend of mine, with bags and pens for one of his customers.

His customer also wanted polo shirts and the same state of affairs as the memory sticks followed. The customer could get them cheaper elsewhere and so he went elsewhere.

I spoke to Graham and he said something along the lines of...

"Hi Mo, do you remember that customer who we did the bags and pens for and he went somewhere else for his polos? Well, he called me yesterday and complained that his polos were printed with a spelling mistake. He asked me what I was going to do about it and I said 'Nothing, you didn't have them from us, you went with someone cheaper.'"

Funny thing is, if we had supplied his polo shirts he'd have been covered by our guarantee, so even if it were his mistake, we'd have replaced them for free.

Now, I genuinely don't like it when people have a bad experience, and I do feel for them when things go wrong. But I have to admit that I have no sympathy for anyone who buys on price alone and then gets upset when things go wrong.

Finally when you have all your samples, show them to other people, get their views and even let them try them out for you. Remember though, although their opinion is useful, it's up to *you* to make the final decision.

Step 6 - Make your final selection

Within a day or so your range will be almost there.

You're likely to find that one or two products look great in the photos, but when you actually see them they're a bit of a let down. So allow a bit more time to plug any holes in your range.

We always recommend you order the minimum when you're buying new products – just the number that you need to get by. This is just in case they don't go down as well as you expected. They may cost a few pennies more per item, but the overall cost will be lower and, like anything new you try for the first time, you never know how successful it'll be until you test it.

A great little exercise you can do to stand out from the crowd:

Ok, so here's my great little exercise to help you be different from your competitors.

→ Write down all the procedures you have in your company. Start with how you answer the phone and what you say, and go right through to your sales process and after sales activity. Also, include the different methods you use to get new business.

→ Then, next to each procedure, write down another way of doing it that most companies probably don't (or won't) do because it takes more effort. They only have to be tiny changes (go the extra inch, remember) and the differences they'll make will make you stand out from the crowd.

Here are just two of many examples we've put in place:

1. When someone calls for the first time and wants to email us a design they have, or an image they want us to see, rather than giving *them* our email address, we ask them for *theirs* and we email them so they can simply hit reply rather than having to type in an address. This may seem unimportant but anything you can do, no matter how small, to make things easier for a customer or prospect is huge.

2. Unlike many of our competitors who either charge for samples above a certain value or loan them (*"if you don't return them, we'll charge you"*), we make a point of telling people to keep them. We also encourage them to try them out, show them around and let us have some feedback.

KEY TAKE AWAY POINTS ARE:

- ✓ **Good customer service is the bare minimum** – Look at ways you can wow your customers or clients.

- ✓ **Be different** – Look at what your competitors are doing and do the opposite.

- ✓ **Create an ideas database** – It'll save you time in the long run.

- ✓ **Planning** - Schedule ahead rather than leaving things to the last minute.

CHAPTER 3

The Seven Motives for Investing in Promotional Products

We touched on the main purposes of investing in promotional products in Chapter 1. Now we'll go a bit deeper and look at the main reasons to invest, and the most effective strategies and tactics you can use to make your promotional items work harder for you.

The 7 Motives Explained

Motive #1 - To create awareness

Why does any company need to create awareness?

Because if the people who you want to do business with aren't aware of you, they can't do business with you. Sounds a bit obvious, but you'd be surprised at the number of businesses that don't get it.

Ever noticed how that new restaurant you went to a few months ago that you really liked suddenly shut down? And it's not just new companies that fail. How about the company you used to do business with ages ago, but you just can't remember their name anymore, so you can't give them business?

You could have the best products in the world and offer a service that is second to none, but if nobody knows who you are or they can't remember you, they can't buy from you. Getting your name out there and keeping it in the front of people's minds is crucial to the success of any company, and it's not as difficult as you may think.

We know how simply buying thousands of cheap plastic pens and handing them out to all and sundry in the hope people will notice your name and suddenly jump on your website or pick up the phone and call you isn't going to happen in a million years.

I'm not saying you shouldn't invest in promotional pens, as long as they don't look cheap and are a bit different, as I mentioned in Chapter 1. They do, however, have their place and can help to bring a prospect closer to making a purchase.

What's also important to understand is that creating awareness won't necessarily generate business for you immediately, but it will keep your name in front of the people you want to do business with, so that when they need your products or services, they'll think of you before your competitors. They'll also know how to get in touch with you.

So, let's look at an example of how, with the help of promotional products, you can make someone aware of your company and, more importantly, allow you to contact them.

If you're exhibiting at a trade show, choose a product that's different but relevant to your business. If you're an IT company, for example, it could be a Power Bank or device charging cable. Hand them out to people at the exhibition who show genuine interest in doing business with you in return for the promise of accepting a phone call from you a few days later. Even go as far as booking it in your calendar in their presence.

When you do call them, they'll remember you above most other people they met because you're the guy who gave them something useful and of genuine value.

Motive # 2 - To attract the right audience

Believe it or not, it's just as important to push away the people you don't want to do business with as it is to attract the people you do want to do business with.

You're not alone: we all have customers from hell.

They're the 20% of customers that swallow up a disproportionate amount of your time. They beat you down on price, constantly complain and you always have to chase them for money. Sound familiar?

Now, imagine how much better your life would be if you didn't have to deal with them. How every customer or client would be a joy to deal with and how, because of all the additional time you had, you could really look after the customers that are important to you.

It's actually quite easy to achieve – you simply sack them. We do it all the time (in a kind and helpful way, of course), and our lives are so much better because of this.

Anyway, attracting the right audience - the people that are a good fit for you and your company - with the help of promotional products is quite simple

First, you need to decide who is your perfect customer - we covered this in Chapter 2 when I showed you how to create your avatar. If you'd like to see how we created ours, it's on the website www.promopowersupremacy.co.uk. You could also create an avatar of the person you don't want to do business with. (Although this isn't essential, it can be great fun and will help.)

Then it's a question of making sure the products you choose match your ideal customer profile.

What you'll find is that your ideal customer or client is actually very similar to you. It's human nature to be attracted to people who are similar to each other and have stuff in common.

GREAT LITTLE TIP

I touched on this in Chapter 1, but just to get the point across: when you're choosing promotional products, select stuff you like yourself. One of the reasons why Apple is the biggest company in the world is because they make products that appeal to them, rather than trying to work out what would appeal to their customers.

Here's an email we use in a nurturing campaign, which targets prospects who have been in touch with us. It kind of pushes away the people we don't want, such as price buyers (let's face it, who does love price buyers?), while attracting people who are a good fit.

Here are 6 Reasons NOT to choose us

You've probably read a few *'reasons to...'* articles and *'why you should choose us'* emails, so I thought I'd give you six reasons NOT to choose us, purely because we really go out of our way to be distinctly different to others.

1. Our products are too expensive

This is true if you're looking for the cheapest possible price and don't value or can't afford the luxury of knowing your order is in safe hands and that it'll be delivered on time whatever hiccups there are along the way.

2. We don't offer the really cheap options like our competitors do

Quality counts and while it's tempting to buy the cheapest possible promotional product to use in your campaign, this choice may come back to haunt you.

Your customer or prospect will form an opinion of your company based on the quality of the gift you send them and if, for example, you send them a pen that doesn't write well or a printed T-shirt that fades in the first wash, they will subconsciously assume that the company they received the gift from is low quality too.

3. You can't see what you're looking for on our website

Business technology and IT continues to expand and improve at an extraordinary rate, and new products and ideas are arriving on the scene faster than ever before. For that reason, not every product available is shown on our website. So, as the saying goes, "if you can't see what you're looking for, please ask".

4. We're just the same as all the others

Perhaps. We deliver your goods, and that's what all good

suppliers do, but... how many companies will ask you questions to make sure you don't choose the wrong product? How many want to give you what's best for you rather than them? How many have a guarantee protecting you and ensuring you are given a product you're totally delighted with?

5. We don't do the huge discounts some suppliers do

Have you ever wondered why some suppliers do this? Could it be because they really like you? Maybe it's because they're making so much money they want to share some of it with you. Or maybe it's because they really need the work and are so desperate they're prepared to offer their products and services at almost cost price just to keep busy.

Only they know the answer, but in times of shortage my humble opinion is that giving more for the same is better than giving the same for less. Giving a more improved service, giving more of the product for the same price, even giving a more superior item for the same price.

6. I don't know them well enough to trust them

And why should you trust anyone if you don't know anything about them?

Some businesses, even today, still think that making the sale is the big thing. In fact, too many businesses still have the attitude that getting an order whatever it takes is all that matters. And, if the customer comes back, that's a bonus.

The big thing for me is building long-term relationships. If I said it's because I'm short of best friends, I'd be lying. The truth is that if I gain your trust you may give me the chance to help you, and if my team and I deliver on our promises to you, which we almost always do, we'll make your life easier and you'll hopefully come back again and again.

Motive #3 - To help start a meaningful relationship

A big mistake people make, and this applies not just to promotional products but to most marketing strategies and tactics, is failing to have a clear end action. They haven't worked out what they want to achieve or the steps required to get there.

Let me give you an example...

A company is exhibiting at a trade show and when asked why they're doing it or what they want to get from it, they say, *"We want more customers."* They're then asked how they're going to get more customers by exhibiting at the show. They reply, *"We're just going to talk to people and offer them our services."*

This is so wrong.

Think about it.

You meet a total stranger who has never heard of you and you try to sell him your products or services. Chances are, as you already know, he's one of the 97% of people who are just looking and not ready to buy. So you grab his business card, hand him a cheap pen or a plastic keyring together with your glossy brochure, and he promises you he'll be in touch.

Trouble is, your glossy brochure and cheap promotional products will never even leave the exhibition. Instead, they'll end up with all the other glossy brochures - in the bin at the exit. Or, if you're really lucky, they might make it to his office where they'll be shoved in the corner with all the other brochures, pens and key rings. A few months later, they'll finish up in the bin.

Here's a better way.

Break it down into a few *'wins'* that'll lead up to making the sale.

So, first decide what you want your potential customer to do to start the relationship and the steps or 'wins' needed to build the trust. It could be something like this...

Here are the three wins to making the sale:

1. Getting them to agree to a phone call

The first thing you need to do, and this is important, is to qualify them. There's no point spending precious time on someone who won't benefit from your products, or isn't a good fit. So ask questions first.

Then, just as I covered at the beginning of this chapter, if they qualify explain that you think they'll benefit from your products and you'd like to give them one of your promotional items, which is useful and of high value, in return for a scheduled call. And, as I mentioned before, even go as far as booking it in your calendar in their presence.

2. Getting them to agree to a meeting or presentation

So, you have a scheduled meeting with them, which means you have their undivided attention for the 15 or 20 minutes of the call. You mentioned at the show that the purpose of the call was to arrange a presentation date, so ask them a few more questions that will enable you to tailor your presentation to address their problems, with the solution just happening to be the products and services you offer.

3. The meeting

You're almost home and dry. All you need to do now is convert them into a paying customer

Remember, you've qualified them, you know exactly what their problems are, and you have the perfect solution. Make your presentation all about them. Cover the challenges they have, address any objections and show them the solutions to their problem.

At the end of the presentation, **don't be afraid to ask this question:** *"What has to happen now for us to be able to do business together?"*

Motive #4 - To get new business

Getting new business is not the easiest thing to do, and without a regular stream of new customers or clients, a company will almost certainly fail.

Cold calling is painful, time consuming and, in my opinion, a total waste of time. First, you need to get past the gatekeeper. If you're lucky enough to do that, you need to convince someone who hasn't a clue who you are that your products or services are better than anyone else's. And if you manage to do that, which is highly unlikely, chances are they're not actually looking for what you have to offer at the time you call them.

So when they say things like, *"Oh, send me an email about what you do,"* or, *"I'll be in touch if I need your stuff,"* what they actually mean is: *"I haven't got a clue who you are and therefore have no intention of buying your products and I just want to get you off the phone as fast as I can."*

Personally I won't talk to anyone I don't know who calls up out of the blue. I don't want them wasting their time and nor do I want them wasting mine. I'm sure you agree.

Interesting stats about cold calling:

Here are some interesting stats, just to show you how much of a waste of time, money and effort cold calling really is.

- 3% of potential buyers at any given time are buying right now

- 6-7% are open to the idea of buying

- 30% are not thinking about it. So they're not against it or for it; they're just not thinking about it

- 30% don't think they're interested

- 30% are definitely not interested

So, when you get on the phone to cold call a list of people, a whopping 97% are not interested, at that precise time, in what you have to offer.

Now there is a way to get new business by cold calling a list of people who you've never spoken to before. They'll be more than happy to chat to you and possibly do business with you too.

Here's a great example of how you can get new business with the help of promotional products.

1. **Create a list of people** – Simply write down all the companies you'd really love to do business with - your dream clients or customers.

2. **Send something in the post** – They call it 'lumpy mail' in America. Just choose something that'll get them to take notice.

3. **Call them** – Because you've sent them something in the post (that's unusual or different) it's not the same as cold calling and they will speak to you.

Introduce yourself as the person who sent this random item in the post and then explain the reason why you did it.

I'll tell you about my Zombie Juggling Balls when I go into more detail about the process and walk you through it in Chapter 4.

Motive # 5 - To get someone to buy from you – ethically

You owe it to your customers and prospects to sell to them.

When you think about it, you have a great product or service and there are people who will benefit hugely from using it.

Trouble is, you have to convince them of this and that's not the easiest thing to do.

There are many emotional triggers you can use and, as long as you use them ethically, I personally see no reason why you shouldn't take advantage of them. And besides, when these emotional tools are used unethically, any short-term gains will almost invariably be followed by long-term losses.

In his book, *Influence: The Psychology of Persuasion*, Robert Cialdini explains this brilliantly. His Six Principles of Persuasion include the rule of reciprocation, which basically means people feel indebted to those who do something for them or give them a gift.

So, giving a customer or prospect a goody bag full of promotional products at a seminar or a useful item after a sales pitch will make them feel like they should return the favour somehow.

Here's a true story I emailed my list a while ago. It shows the rule of reciprocation working (because my customer had given me so much business, when she asked for a discount, I simply couldn't say no).

Ever been hit by the rule of reciprocation?

Yesterday, I was caught by the rule of reciprocation and it actually felt good.

The rule of reciprocation, as explained by Robert Cialdini in his brilliant book, *'Influence: The Psychology of Persuasion'*, says:

"As humans, we generally aim to return favours, pay back debts and treat others as they treat us.

According to the idea of reciprocity, this can lead us to feel obliged to offer concessions or discounts to others if they have offered them to us.

It's human nature to want to give something, in return, to someone who has given."

Here's how I got caught and the surprise reaction I received.

I'd almost completed a frenzied buying session with a customer (and because of the time we've known each other, a really good friend too). It was frenzied because there were a lot of products involved, deadlines were looming and a key person involved was due to go on holiday.

So with all but a small number of products left to order, my customer asked if I could look at reducing the price on a product because she preferred the higher priced item but her budget didn't stretch.

Now the orders she'd placed so far were substantial, so I emailed her:

"Hi Sara,

The supplier can't reduce the price but I can come down to 19p each if it helps...

... you've given me so much business I don't mind doing them for whatever you want to pay."

And Sara's reply:

"You are not a charity, Mo.

19p is great!"

Don't you just love customers like Sara?

By the way...

The latest few products we've managed to track down for Sara are: cartons of coconut water (I love coconut water), a stretchy, camo print chair and table covers, camo face paint and bars of chocolate coated with coconut ice.

You see, I offered a discount almost straightaway as I felt she had given me so much business and I really wanted to willingly give her something back in return. Interestingly, when I suggested, *"I don't mind doing them for whatever you want to pay,"* she replied, *"You are not a charity, Mo..."* She was kind of offering it right back, by agreeing to 19p when what she really wanted to pay (I suspect) was much less. Try it yourself sometime, it works!

Motive #6 - To thank them for doing business with you

As I mentioned in Chapter 1, sending a thank you gift to a customer or client for doing business with you is 'huge', and I really don't understand why most businesses don't do this.

When I say 'huge', I mean it shows you appreciate their business, it helps them remember you and it's a vital part of your after sales follow-up process.

Here's another of my regular emails that sums this up nicely.

One of those tumbleweed moments

One of the things I've noticed when doing business with people is that they never really say thank you.

There's always lots of activity: phone calls, emails, more phone calls, even more emails and then that's it, job done, service completed, goods delivered and then... nothing.

You could hear tumbleweed gently rolling past you, a pin drop and the sound of crickets rubbing their little legs together.

For some strange reason, a supplier will suddenly stop all contact after a service is complete or a product delivered. The message this gives to the customer is probably: "They've had their money and now they're not interested anymore."

Maybe it's not totally conscious, maybe they're not thinking it at the time, but the next time you contact them a couple of months later, don't seem surprised if they assume you're calling them for only one reason.

Now here are some really easy, quick and simple things you can do to ensure your customers appreciate you as much as you appreciate them.

Send them a thank you gift a week or so after the order or service has been completed - they won't be expecting it and they will remember you.

Call them just to make sure they were happy with everything and ask how the service or product was received by others. Showing an interest in them and what your product did to enhance their position or reputation will make them feel good.

Ask them if there's anything else you can help them with either now or in the near future - if they're delighted with what you've done to help them, they will want to give you more.

Everyone who uses our products and services gets a little gift in the post after their first order with us (if for any reason you haven't had yours, let me know and I'll pop one in the post today), all wrapped in paper and printed with thank you in a dozen or so different languages.

So, if you'd like some help and advice choosing a great thank you gift for your customers, hit reply, give me a brief idea of what you do and I'll make sure you have a selection to look at within a day or two.

GREAT LITTLE TIP

It goes without saying that the thank you gift you send will be useful and something your customer will use often, but it will be even more special if you personalise it. Even printing out a wrapper with their name on it has a far more intimate meaning.

Motive #7 - To get them to come back again and again

There's only one way you can ensure your customers keep coming back, and it's so obvious I really don't know why all companies don't do it.

Keep in touch with them.

When you think about it, your customer list is a gold mine. Getting new customers costs money on advertising and it costs time because you need to develop the relationship that leads to the sale. Whereas you've 'paid' for your customer and selling more to them is actually easier than you may think.

Most companies spend all their time and effort chasing new customers: they miss all the business sitting right there under their noses.

Here are three ways to keep in touch with your customers, so it's you they remember rather than your competitors when they need your products or services.

1. Create an after sales campaign when someone orders from you for the first time. This can include:

- ✓ An email asking them to complete a short *"How did we do?"* survey.

- ✓ A phone call to thank them for the business and to ask a few questions, such as, when they may need your help in the future and if there's anyone they know who may benefit from your products or services.

- ✓ Ask for a testimonial – you can use them in the footer of your emails, on your website and in your marketing campaigns.

✓ Send them a thank you gift for placing an order with you.
It doesn't have to cost much - it's the thought that counts.

2. Send them regular emails.

Contrary to what you might think, people are more than happy
to receive regular emails from you, as long as you are not
constantly trying to sell to them.

Interestingly, my unsubscribe rate changed from around
0.9% when I emailed our customers and prospects weekly to
0.06% when I sent them emails every day, and that's from a list
of over 2,500 contacts.

3. Send them a little something from time to time.

Customers are not just for Christmas, so rather than just
sending them a gift at that time of year (which probably gets
lumped together with all the other gifts they receive and
therefore has little impact), surprise them with a little
something during Valentine's or Easter.

One year for Valentine's Day, we sent our top customers
either giant heart-shaped personalised cookies or chocolates.
They went down a storm.

Figure 11: Image of Heart Shaped Cookie and Chocolates

KEY TAKE AWAY POINTS ARE:

- ✓ **Decide who you want to do business with** – It'll save you wasting your time on people you'd rather avoid.

- ✓ **Choose promotional products you would like to receive yourself** – It'll help to attract the people you want to do business with.

- ✓ **Avoid cold calling** – Warm them up first.

- ✓ **Send your customers small gifts at times when they'll least expect them** – They'll mean a lot more.

CHAPTER 4

The Dream 100 Concept

What is the Dream 100 Concept?

Created and perfected by Chet Holmes, who has been described by people he's worked with as one of the best marketers on the planet, the *Dream 100 Concept* is probably one of the most powerful ways to attract and do business with the biggest companies in your industry. His book, *'The Ultimate Sales Machine'*, goes into the concept in depth and shows, through examples, how easily anyone in any B2B company can double their turnover simply by following strategies and tactics.

Simply put, the Dream 100 Concept filters your potential client list down to the few people you really should be doing business with - the crème de la crème, the best of the best, the big spenders - and converts them into buying customers.

One great example he writes about is how he helped a magazine publisher dramatically increase their revenue in just six weeks. Here's how he did it...

The fastest way to build your business is to target the best clients

His client was the 15th biggest magazine publisher in the US, and their list of potential advertisers totalled 2,200. They would regularly target the entire list but their direct mail marketing campaigns and follow-ups were wimpy and weak. The results were poor. So Chet Holmes ran an analysis of the list and discovered (in typical 80/20 fashion) that 167 of them bought 95% of all the advertising in that industry. Interestingly, but not surprisingly, they didn't have a single client from those top spenders.

So they stopped targeting the entire list and instead spent the same monthly budget focusing relentlessly on the top 8%. This meant they were able to use a stacked marketing approach – getting all the different marketing weapons to work together (I explain this later in the chapter). Within six months, they had 29 of the top spenders.

Running a Dream 100 campaign is simple although not necessarily easy, as it does take focus and a bit of effort. Here are two things you need to know.

1. **Be relentless and don't give up** – It's very common for someone to send out a direct mail piece or phone people on a list, get zero results and give up. What you need to be aware of is that every time you make contact you bring your prospect closer to becoming a paying customer - so don't give up easily.

2. **Understand what success actually is** –It's very easy to think that the results you achieve from a campaign are insignificant and therefore not worth continuing.

Here's an example:

Chet Holmes created a telephone script for a top sales guy and the following week he had a conference call with the entire staff, including the CEO, to discuss the results. The conversation went something like this:

CHET: *So, how did it go?*

SALES GUY: *It didn't work.*

CHET: *It didn't work?*

SALES GUY: *No, it didn't work.*

CHET: *How many people did you offer it to?*

SALES GUY: *I offered it to 10 people.*

CHET: *And nobody bought it?*

SALES GUY: *No, two people bought it.*

Now, the thing is, the sales guy, when looking at the results, saw that almost everyone he called didn't buy. Eight no thank yous out of 10 made the campaign a failure.

But think about it. If you call, say, 100 people every week and 20 people buy, that's a whopping 1,000-plus additional sales a year.

I've spoken to so many people who created a campaign, tried it once, deemed it a failure because it didn't generate huge amounts of business and then scrapped it.

The 3 simple stages to turn the companies you dream about doing business with into companies you actually do business with:

Imagine this. You take three simple stages and within a few weeks you're actually doing business with those companies you never thought you'd have a hope in hell of doing business with.

It's actually really simple and, as long as you're prepared to put in a little time and effort, it'll work in your company too. So, let's have a quick look at the three simple stages before we go into the nitty-gritty detail.

Stage 1: Choose the companies you want to do business with – Although we call this the Dream 100 Concept because in most B2B industries there are at least 100 top spenders, I suggest targeting 50. This is because it's a number you can easily focus on and manage. Also, so you can budget better, test and measure the results and refine your campaign for next time.

Stage 2: Choose your products – This is the fun bit. Choose four items you can send them in the post and create a theme around each product. An example is my Zombie Juggling Balls and the theme, "Don't Let Your Customers Think You're No Longer in the Land of the Living!

Stage 3: Create your Dream 100 campaign – I call it the '*3 step and repeat 4 times*' campaign, because we repeat the process, which contains three steps, four times. It's all about being relentless and not giving up too easily. We'll also be using the stacked marketing approach, which is a combination of direct mail, phone calls and emails.

The Dream 100 Strategy

So, how can you target the biggest potential clients in your industry and within a few weeks start doing business with them? Simple - by putting the Dream 100 Concept to work in your business. I'm going to walk you through the strategy and tactics I personally use in my business, which will work just as successfully for any B2B company, regardless of their industry (there may be the odd exception, but I can't think of one). This campaign can be easily implemented in your business. So, let's get started.

The preliminary thing you need to do is put together your strategy. So, let's say, like me, your strategy is to call up the biggest companies that have a need for your products or services, speak to the buyer, arrange a meeting and after the meeting get them to start buying from you. Sounds difficult, if not impossible? It's actually easier than you think.

Stage 1: Choose the companies you want to do business with

The first thing is to choose the companies you would love to do business with, the companies you dream about working with. Choose no more than 50, anymore and you won't be able to spend the time needed to make this work effectively. Then you need to find the best person to get in touch with, which is a lot easier than you may think.

Start by typing the company name and job title of the person you need to find into Google and LinkedIn. This is likely to flag up more than one person, so either add the one who you think is most likely to be correct, or add more than one contact. Once you've completed your list, you then need to verify the details.

The information on the internet could be out of date as people move jobs and it doesn't always get updated, so simply call up the companies and ask them. Just say you want to send something in the post to the person responsible for buying your product and you want to make sure the name you have is the best person to send it to. Because you already have a contact name and just want to confirm it's correct, you'll find the person on the other end of the phone will be more helpful as your call doesn't come across as a blatant cold call.

When I did it, most people were really helpful and either confirmed the name I had was correct or suggested a better contact. A few people were a bit cagey and weren't prepared to divulge such confidential, life threatening information, and in those instances I just crossed them off the list and moved on.

Stage 2: Choose your products and your Call to Action

Ok, so you have your list of contacts for the 50 companies you dream of doing business with and you've verified their details.

This is where all the fun comes in. You now need to choose four different products you'll be sending them in the post and create a theme around each one. What's really important here is that the items need to be different so they'll get noticed and be a talking point in the office. Here are three of the products I've chosen for my campaign...

The first are *Zombie Juggling Balls* and a headline that says: ***"Don't Let Your Customers Think You're No Longer in the Land of the Living!"*** The theme here is all about reminding your customers that you're still around and you haven't disappeared into the land of the walking dead. We really went to town on this one and created (painfully by hand) special tubes to send them in. Have a look at how cool they look in figure 12.

Figure 12: Zombie Juggling Balls

Second up is a breath freshener spray with the headline: ***"Don't Allow Your Customers to Think You Pong."*** What we're getting across here is how important it is to use an expert rather than doing it alone: *"Get it wrong and your customers and prospects are likely to think your company stinks. Get it right and you'll keep your name fresh in the minds of your customers and prospects."* Just to add to the fun, the label on the bottle has the words *"Customer Attraction Spray"*.

The third item is a Power Bank in the shape of a credit card. The headline reads: ***"Keeping You Connected With Your Customers."*** Here we're showing how important it is to stay in touch with your customers or clients by as many means as possible, and keeping the campaign charged.

Next, you need to decide exactly what you want them to do. What's the most important thing you can get them to do that leads to a sale? It could be getting them to watch a webinar, attend a workshop or sign up to a free report. For us, the one thing that almost always guarantees us a sale is our Personalised Product Catalogue service, and for that we need a conversation on the phone to fully explain the benefits. So our Call to Action is to get them to call us so we can start a conversation.

GREAT LITTLE TIP

Give them a compelling reason to take the action you want them to. Something like, *"I know your time is precious so my guarantee to you is this: If you don't see any benefit after our scheduled call, I will personally give you a voucher for £50 to spend in almost any retail store in the UK."*

Before I go any further, let me remind you what I said in chapter 3 (page 81). Cold calling is a complete waste of time. Remember, 97% of the people you call are not interested in buying at the time you call them... it doesn't make sense to waste your time trying to convince them otherwise. Instead, use the tactic I'm sharing now – it'll be much more effective.

Stage 3: Create your Dream 100 campaign

You now need to create your '3 step and repeat 4 times' campaign (this will make more sense as we go along), and you'll be using all the marketing weapons available to you in the stacked marketing approach. So, let's go through each step carefully.

Step 1 – Write your letters

First, write your letters. Start with your headline to grab their attention then tell them why you've sent them something in the post.

An example of how you can start your letters could be something like this:

Dear [First_Name],

Don't Let Your Customers Think You're No Longer in the Land of the Living!

You're probably looking at your set of Zombie Juggling Balls and wondering why anyone in their right mind would ever send you something so random and so odd.

So let me be totally honest and upfront and tell you why.

Don't forget your Call to Action. If you want them to call you, then tell them the best time and the best number to get you on. Surprisingly, one person on my list did call, we arranged a scheduled call, arranged a meeting and now she's a buying customer. (I say surprisingly because, from experience, I didn't think I'd get a reaction so early on in the campaign.)

You can see all the letters I've used on the website.
www.promopowersupremacy.co.uk

Step 2 – Call them

You have less than five seconds to make an impression when you speak to someone on the phone for the first time, so, before you pick up the phone, write a script and read it out aloud as many times as you need to in order to remember it pretty much word for word.

Include in your script what to say to the *'gatekeeper'* if you don't get straight through to the person you want to speak to. When they ask who you are and why you're calling simply say what I say: *"My name's Mo, I sent Doris a few items in the post and I'm just making sure they arrived safely."* If Doris is available, you'll get put through almost every time.

Then all you need to say to Doris is: *"Hi Doris, I'm the guy who sent you the Zombie Juggling Balls, did they arrive with you Ok?"*

An email I sent to my list shows just how powerful this tactic is...

They laughed at my Zombie Juggling Balls

Imagine calling someone you don't know and, as soon as you've explained who you are, they laugh.

This happened to me last week, three times in fact, and it was exactly the reaction I was hoping for.

It's all part of my new Dream 100 campaign. I send my list of people I dream of doing business with something a bit out of the ordinary in the post to grab their attention, and then I phone them.

Actually, I've sent two things so far: Zombie Juggling Balls and Breath Freshener, but I think it was the juggling balls that really made them laugh.

Now, before you think I'm totally mad, let me explain why I'm doing it.

We all know cold calling doesn't work. It's painful to do and generally people don't like receiving calls from strangers. I personally don't speak to people who call trying to sell me stuff. I don't want to waste their time and besides, when I want something, I'll ask around.

Sending something random in the post and creating a theme around it (the letter I sent out with the breath freshener had the headline *"Don't Let Your Customers Think You Stink!"*), means when you call them, they'll know who you are and will be more inclined to talk to you. In fact, you'll find they'll want to know more about you and what you do.

So far we have meetings planned with two companies and an almost confirmed order. And the really great thing is... the campaign still has a month or so to run.

Now, although it's a very simple and easy way to get new business, you do have to put the hard work in. Unless, that is, you'd like me to do the hard work for you.

Want more customers or clients? Want me to help you get them?

Simply click the link and I'll tell you more... I'd like to know more about how you can help me do business with the companies I dream of doing business with.

P.S. One of the companies on my list is a well-known British airline. I easily managed to speak to the person who's responsible for promotional products (she actually laughed at me too). On this occasion, though, I wasn't lucky. She said something about having a Rostered Agency System, which meant we couldn't help her. Oh well, can't win 'em all.

Step 3 – Write your emails

There will be some people who you just won't be able to get through to by phone, so your final step is to send a personal email.

It's important you send them individually from your email client, rather than an autoresponder or other bulk email system. This will help prevent them being treated as spam.

In your email, start by saying you're the person who sent the random items in the post and why you're sending them an email. Mention that you tried calling a few times and it is not your intention to spam them. Then make your offer and tell them what you want them to do. Just like your letters, write a different one ready to send after each product has been sent and phone calls have been made.

GREAT LITTLE TIP

Include your email address in a link and offer times for you to call them. Something like this...

"...Please click the email link and type the best number to reach you on and also when, by typing in "this morning", "this afternoon" or "tomorrow morning". The call will last no more than three minutes... Here's the link."

Alternatively you could use scheduling appointment software such as Calendly.

Now you are ready to start your '3 step and repeat 4 times' campaign.

Here's how it all fits together:

→ **Week 1 - Send out your first item and letter** – I send

mine out on Fridays so they arrive early in the week. No real reason other than I can make the phone calls the same week they're received. Send them either first class or recorded delivery so you know they should arrive the next day.

→ **Week 2 - Call them** – Avoid Mondays. No one likes getting phone calls from relative strangers on the first day back at work after the weekend. Make sure you make your calls no later than a week or so after you send them, the longer you wait, the less effective they'll be. Call three times before giving up.

→ **Week 3 - Email them** – Avoid Fridays. Some people will be rushing to get their week's work finished, or they'll be thinking about the weekend. Tuesday is possibly a good day to send them and people tend to respond better to emails before 11:00am. Why? I haven't a clue, but do test different days and times if you want to.

→ **Week 4 - Repeat the three steps** – It's important to keep the momentum going. Just like most things we do in marketing, the more you do and the more persistent you are, the more successful your campaigns will be.

So for this to work, you really do need to repeat the tactics again, and again, and again. Hence the name *'3 step and repeat 4 times'* campaign.

KEY TAKE AWAY POINTS ARE:

- ✔ **Be relentless** – Every time you make contact you bring your prospect closer to becoming a paying customer.

- ✔ **Understand what success actually is** – Your campaign doesn't need to generate huge amounts of money straightaway.

- ✔ **Give them a compelling reason to take action** – If your prospect doesn't see any benefit to them, they won't take the action you want them to.

- ✔ **Don't forget your Call to Action** – Tell your prospect exactly what you want them to do. If you don't, how will they know?

CHAPTER 5

Promotional Products in Action

Real Life Examples of How Promotional Products Have Worked Incredibly Well

In this chapter, we're going to look at the strategies and tactics behind several successful campaigns and see just how effective they were. I'll also show you how easily you can copy or adapt these campaigns and put them to work in your company.

As we covered in Chapter 1, there are lots of different reasons for investing in promotional products, and although sometimes it can be difficult to measure, in terms of hard cash earned, they can achieve amazing results, which will ultimately lead to more revenue and bigger profits.

Remember, the main purpose of investing in promotional items is to create awareness of your company's services or products, to stand out above your competitors and to stay top of mind with your customers so it's you they'll come back to when they need the products or services you offer.

We'll cover *five different campaigns*. The first is covered in a lot of detail because it's something I've personally created, and the others will explain a bit about the objectives and results achieved.

So, let's get started with a campaign every B2B company that has customers who buy regularly can copy. It's also a particular favourite of mine.

Promotional products in action #1 – Mo's lapsed customer campaign

We repeat this campaign on a regular basis because it does exactly what we want it to do... it brings back customers who, for whatever reason, stopped using our services.

We've tested various tactics: some have worked incredibly well, such as the boomerang in the post approach (more about that shortly), and others not so well. The lapsed customer campaign I'm sharing with you now is the tried, tested and polished version that, in my opinion, will give you the best results.

There are three phases to the campaign, so let's have a look and see just how easy it is to set up and get working in your company.

Phase 1 – Identify your lapsed customers

First up is to identify not just who your lapsed customers are, but also the ones who are worth spending the time, effort and money to win back. There may be little point in targeting someone who spent a small amount with you once and is unlikely to benefit from your products or services again. Then create the criteria of the people you want to target. It could be people who've bought more than once a year and spend a minimum of, say, £1,000.

Once you've done that, identify your lapsed customers. If you're a hairdresser, for example, it could be someone who hasn't been to see you for three months. For a garage owner it could be someone who hasn't had his or her car serviced for over a year. For me, it's a client we haven't helped for 18 months.

When you have your list of lapsed customers you need to call them to make sure the information you have is still correct. Some may have stopped trading, some may have moved premises and some of the contacts could have changed. You now have an accurate and highly-qualified list of people to target.

Phase 2 – Your Call to Action and offer

This is the most important part of the campaign. Without a Call to Action and an offer, it will fail miserably, so, before you do anything else, decide what you want them to do and what you'll give them in return.

What works for us is to offer a money-off voucher, which they can claim by going onto a webpage and leaving their details so that we can then contact them again at a later date. (Or create a separate email campaign. I'll explain that in more detail later.)

Phase 3 – Build your campaign

There are three easy stages to the perfect lapsed customer campaign.

1. **Create a personalised postcard:** It's very easy and cost effective these days to print up and send out postcards, so even if your list of lapsed customers is 50 or less, don't worry, this campaign will still be effective and should still give you a good return on investment.

It's important to personalise your postcard, so make sure you address the person by their first name. As with most marketing copy, start with a headline to attract their attention and then make sure your first sentence draws them in and compels them to continue reading. So, something like this...

Haven't Seen You For A While... Was It Something I Did?

Hi {FIRST_NAME},

I haven't heard from you for ages and I can't bear the thought of even more time passing by without you...

Also, don't forget your Call to Action. It could be for them to claim a money-off voucher or a free gift, but you do need to get them to take some sort of action.

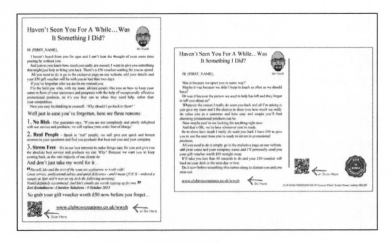

Figure 13: Mo's lapsed customer postcard

GREAT LITTLE TIP

Have the same message both sides but worded differently, so that certain words and phrases you use will strike a chord with more people. Also, it'll be immediately clear what your message is, whatever side they look at first.

2. **Create your shock and awe package:** You might find the uptake from your postcard to be tiny. From a list of around 100, we would typically get one or two responses, so don't be disappointed if the response is small, you're simply warming them up for what comes next, which is your shock and awe package.

Next up, you need to create the first shock and awe package, which is basically a plastic boomerang and a few sheets of paper.

Get some plastic boomerangs printed up with the words *"We Really Do Want You to Come Back."* Then stick the boomerang to a sheet of paper, which will mean as soon as they see it, the reason you've sent it will be clear. And, just for a bit of fun, put instructions on how to throw it on the reverse side.

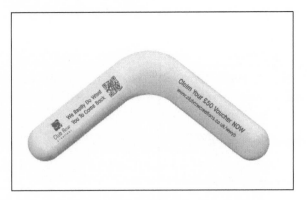

Figure 14: Plastic boomerang with message

Then put together a few useful facts and tips to include in the package, which they'll benefit from. On one sheet have 10 reasons why they should choose you, showing the benefits you can give them that most of your competitors can't. Fill the other side with testimonials, which will strengthen the reasons why they should come back to you. On another sheet, have top tips on how they can get the best out of your products or services. Your final sheet could show one of the services or products on one side and the benefits on the other.

Finally, write your letter and, as with your postcard, you need a headline and a compelling first sentence. Mine starts like this...

Why has this bald fella sent you a boomerang in the post?

Well, let me explain...

Dear {FIRST_NAME},

GREAT LITTLE TIP

Getting someone to actually open an envelope is a challenge in itself, so make it as personal as you can rather than making it obvious it's from a company. So, use a stamp rather than a frank, add the address in a handwriting font and add some copy on your envelope to encourage them to want to open it. Something like *"Special Offer Inside"* works a treat.

I then go on to explain that just like a boomerang, I want them to come back to me.

3. **Launch your campaign:** Before you start this campaign, create the webform you'll be directing them to in order to claim their money-off voucher.

    Then create two email autoresponder campaigns. Anyone who responds by completing the webform will automatically be added to the "responded" campaign and receive an email congratulating them for claiming their voucher. Anyone who doesn't respond will be added manually to the "unresponsive" campaign, where they'll receive an email encouraging them to do so.

Here's how it all fits together:

→   **Week 1 - Send out your postcards** – It's likely the response from the postcard will be small, but don't be disillusioned, this is just the start of the campaign and you're just warming them up. Anyone who does respond by claiming their money-off voucher will, as I mentioned earlier, receive an email congratulating them. Send them a physical voucher in the post and call them a few days later to make sure they have received it.

→ **Week 3 - Send out your shock and awe package –** This will almost certainly get a better response than the postcard. We would typically receive around six to eight voucher requests. As with the postcards, follow up with a phone call a few days after you've sent them their voucher.

→ **Week 4 - Add all those who haven't responded to your 'unresponsive' autoresponder campaign, where they'll receive an email encouraging them to do so -** After this you may decide to give up on the people who haven't replied and either take them off your lists altogether or try again another time.

There is another last-ditch stage you can try and, although I haven't tested it yet, people who've done something similar have reported good results...

Send out to all those who haven't responded a 4-inch plastic bin with a letter inside saying, *"Since You've Thrown Away All My Previous Letters, I Thought This Time I Would Save You The Effort."*

The results

The first time we ran this campaign in 2014, it brought back 12 customers and gave us a return on investment of about 120% in the first three months. Since then we've run three campaigns and the cumulative turnover they've generated is in excess of £30,000.

Promotional products in action #2 – Jan's awareness campaign

Jan West worked in the marketing department at the Riverside Ice & Leisure Centre in Chelmsford.

At weekends they have ice skating disco sessions run by professional DJs. They offer full disco facilities, the latest chart-topping music, lighting, a smoke generator, song requests and even speed skating sessions.

They introduced a new brand called Skateside, and their main target audience were teenagers between the ages of 14 and 17 years. One of their tactics was to hand out flyers. They targeted areas in the town centre where teens would congregate and even gave them out at schools (with permission, of course).

The biggest problem was that teenagers don't do flyers; they're uncool. Getting them to take one was a huge problem.

Jan gave us the challenge of finding a product that would appeal to teenagers, help to create awareness and promote the evening ice skating disco sessions as the new cool place to be.

Jan decided on a logo torch key ring, which, when illuminated, projected their new logo. They attached one to each of their flyers and tried again. The kids went crazy and were queuing to get their hands on them. They became a must-have item. Skateside and the Riverside Ice & Leisure Centre was the coolest place in town.

When I got in touch with Jan to ask her about the campaign she remarked: *"Probably the best promotional goods I've ever been involved with purchasing! A great find there by Wills!"*

The results

The objective was to help raise awareness and portray a cool

113

image of their new brand. Being able to get disruptive teenagers to promote an ice rink, I'd say, was a remarkable achievement.

Riverside confirmed that following this campaign the numbers for the ice skating disco sessions increased and, although it's difficult to quantify the results from the logo torches, they felt they were a contributing factor.

Promotional products in action #3 – Mark's staff retention record

Mark Cottle runs a successful BPO business from the Philippines (BPO stands for Business Process Outsourcing). Basically, he finds and recruits full-time members of staff for Australian and UK businesses.

This is a huge industry and it's still growing at an incredible rate. Mark increased his staff levels in two years from two to over 150, and his growth rate is continuing at a similar pace.

One of the biggest issues BPOs face in the Philippines is staff retention. A typical BPO will turnover between 50% and 100% of its staff over a 12-month period. Think about it. They, in some instances, replace the equivalent of the whole workforce in a year. Imagine the disruption this causes, the stress and hassle of continuously recruiting staff just to stand still and, of course, the costs involved.

Mark's big challenge was how to reduce the need for constantly replacing staff. He worked hard to discover why these retention rates were so poor and put processes in place to make the staff feel important and have a sense of belonging.

One of the ways he achieved this was by organising a team trip once a year. The staff have two days away at a beach resort where they split into teams and participate in competitions against each other. The entertaining and light-hearted rivalry helps to create bonds. Everyone who attends receives a specially printed T-shirt depicting the event. This is huge when it comes to feeling a sense of belonging. The staff wear them with pride and even months and years after the trip, they can still be seen in the office wearing them.

The results

The objective was to improve the poor staff retention rates that are typical in Mark's industry, and although his clever recruiting systems and careful selection of staff is a big contributor, he is in no doubt that the team trips and the company T- shirts the staff wear with pride are large contributing factors.

Most BPOs in the Philippines lose between 50% and 100% of their staff each year. Mark loses less than 10%.

Figure 15: Mark's Team Trip T-Shirts

Promotional products in action #4 – Crispin's warm and fuzzy T-shirts

Crispin works at Brain Tumour Research and one of his many roles involves choosing promotional products.

One of the biggest challenges for all charities is increasing their brand presence, and also getting people actively involved. Crispin says T-shirts have played a big part in achieving these goals.

Brain Tumour Research believes their customers and supporters are the most important part of their organisation; they are also strong advocates of family values.

In addition to other uses, their promotional T-shirts are given away as recognition for an achievement. They are highly sought after and worn with pride (or, as Crispin mentioned to me, when someone wears one on the charity's T-shirts it creates this "warm and fuzzy feeling"). They are also one of the reasons why the charity is growing faster than almost any other medical research charity in the UK.

Their range of striking pink T-shirts have been extended over the last few years to include a kids range, running vests and polo shirts.

The results

The objective was to increase brand presence, get people actively involved and create, through wearing the T-shirts, a sense of belonging.

The demand for the T-shirts has increased at a phenomenal rate; over 400% in the last five years, and is following the same upward trend in growth the charity is enjoying.

Figure 16: Crispin's warm and fuzzy T-shirts

Brain Tumour Research t-shirts are vibrant and unmistakable – even covered in mud, these girls are clearly united and happy to be raising money and awareness for the cause!

Promotional products in action #5 – Mo's Dream 100 campaign

As you know, I covered the Dream 100 Concept in the last chapter. It's an incredibly powerful marketing concept and because of that I feel it deserves another mention here, where I'll share a few additional key details.

We all have customers. Some customers we have are Ok, some are good customers and a small few are our best customers. They are the ones we love working with, the ones we wish we had more of.

Unlike any other marketing strategy I know, the Dream 100 Concept does just that. It doesn't just give you new customers, it gives you those new customers you dream about having.

Google AdWords can generate business, but not necessarily with your dream customers. Again, for some companies,

LinkedIn, Facebook and Twitter are a good way to bring in new customers, but it's also unlikely you'll get those big spending dream customers.

The results

The objective was to attract the people we really wanted to do business with and convert them into customers.

It's still early days, but so far, from a small list of just under 50 companies, we've managed to secure two meetings and had three orders, generating immediate revenue of £2,498. This has already covered the costs of the campaign and a conservative estimate (based on experience and similar patterns in other campaigns), should increase these figures fourfold in the first year and generate regular income from repeat business in future years.

HERE TO HELP...

Do you face any of these challenges in your company? Do you think creating a campaign similar to the ones we've just covered would work in your company? Would you like a helping hand to create one?

Why don't you send me a quick email at mo@clubrowcreations.co.uk. Simply type in the subject line, *"I'd like a bit of help with my campaign,"* hit send and we'll arrange a scheduled chat.

KEY TAKE AWAY POINTS ARE:

✓ **There are many different purposes for creating a marketing campaign** – Make sure you get the message across properly and effectively.

✓ **The main purpose of investing in promotional items is usually to create awareness** – Get this right and the money will follow.

✓ **Investing in promotional products doesn't always need to increase sales** – As in Mark's example, although his team trips and printed T-shirts didn't generate more business, it saved him huge amounts of time, money and hassle on replacing staff.

✓ **Identify the challenge you need to address before you create your campaign** – You'll then be able to tailor it to that specific challenge and achieve far better results.

✓ **Read Chapter 4 again** – Fully understand how the *Dream 100 Concept* works, then implement it in your company.

CHAPTER 6

Marketing Campaigns and How to Make Them Effective

Although this chapter doesn't have much to do with promotional products per se, the marketing campaigns I'll be sharing with you are all part of the marketing mix, and if you invest in promotional products, be it for events, product launches, conferences, seminars or thank you gifts, the information here will be useful and relevant.

Initial Contact and Nurturing

As you know, people buy when they're ready to buy, not when you want them to. They also buy from people they know and trust, so it's important to build the relationship with someone before you start trying to sell to them.

When someone visits your website, for example, most of the time they're just looking. Think of it along the same lines as clothes shopping. You browse from rail to rail and from shop to shop until something catches your eye. You try it on to see if it's a good fit. If you're happy with it, then and only then do you buy.

It's the same when someone's looking for a product or service you can help with. They'll visit a few websites, including yours, and if nothing catches their eye, you've lost them forever. So it's important you grab their attention, and a good way to do this is to offer them something upfront. You could give them a free sample or some free tips relating to your product or service. This is a great way to introduce yourself and start the relationship, as well as showing your expertise at what you do and also that you have their interests at heart.

Something like *'7 Things You Need to Know About [Your Product or Service] Before You Spend a Single Penny'* works particularly well, because you're giving them useful and relevant information about something they're thinking about. Also, the power of reciprocity starts to kick in; if you give someone something, they'll feel obliged to give you something in return.

When someone accepts your free offer they're effectively giving you permission to start a relationship with them, and that's why you need to follow up quickly and relentlessly.

Here's a quick and easy way to start building that relationship:

- ✓ **When someone comes onto your website, offer them some free downloadable tips.** Shoot a quick video explaining why they need to read your tips before they buy, what could happen if they don't and the benefits if they do. Also, explain it with copy: some people prefer to read than watch. Create a webform to capture their details and only ask for the information you require. The less they have to do, the more likely they'll be to respond. I never understand why some companies ask for so much unnecessary information, stuff like: how long you've been in business, how many staff you have, where you live, blahdy, blahdy-blah. Their first name and email address is all you need to ask for.

- ✓ **Once they've downloaded your tips, create an email campaign.** Start by offering them something in the post. It could be a free sample, a little thank you gift for showing an interest in you, or a more detailed bound version of your tips. When they respond, not only will you have their physical address, they'll start trusting you more.

- ✓ **Ask them what their three biggest challenges are that relate to your products and services.** Promise them you'll reply and help them. This is particularly powerful because you can tailor the answer to show how your product or service will fix those challenges.

- ✓ **Call them.** They'll actually appreciate that you've taken the trouble to call them. You can then establish whether they're interested in what you have to offer and also if they're someone you actually want to do business with.

If they're interested but not ready to buy, add them to a nurturing campaign of regular emails.

Turning leads into paying customers

Someone in a business group I'm a member of asked how many times he should follow up when someone enquires about his products. The answer that came back was, *"until they buy, die or beg you to stop."*

Most companies don't follow up enough. They may make a phone call and then a few days later send an email... and then nothing. They assume the prospect is not interested and they stop chasing. I remember years ago, I asked one of my sales guys why he hadn't continuously chased a large enquiry. He said, *"If they were interested, they'd get back to me."* He didn't stay with us for long.

I also found out the hard way, why following up relentlessly is crucial.

It was the beginning of the nineties and, a couple of years earlier, we'd won a big contract to supply ITV with T-shirts and sweatshirts for a telethon they were hosting. After the event, which lasted for almost six months, the coordinator said that of all the suppliers they used, we were by far the best. So when the event came around two years later, I was so sure we would get the contract again that I didn't follow up. I simply quoted the new coordinator and waited for the orders to come flooding in.

We were given the contract for the T-shirts but the rest of the clothing was given to someone else. Luckily for us, that supplier gave an appalling service, the organiser was sacked and we got the business back. Before she so swiftly left, we asked the coordinator why she didn't give us the contract for all the clothing. Her reply was, *"You didn't seem to want the business as much as the other company."*

These days, we follow up relentlessly and our automated system makes it so much easier to do so.

Here's how one of our automated follow up campaigns works.

→ **New prospect enquires** – we add them to an autoresponder, which immediately sends them an email thanking them for enquiring and promising them details and prices shortly.

→ **Follow up #1** – after we've emailed the information, we call them within a day to make sure they have it and we offer free samples. Our autoresponder sends us an email reminding us to do this.

→ **Follow up #2** – two days after sending samples we call them to make sure they have them.

→ **Follow up #3**– four days later they receive an automated email asking if they're still interested and we include an offer of alternative products if they have a tight budget.

→ **Follow up #4** – after another four days, we call them to ask if they're still interested.

→ **Follow up #5** – after a further four days they receive another email offering them a voucher to use on a subsequent order. The offer is only valid for five days.

→ **Follow up #6** – five days later they receive an email reminding them that the offer of a money-off voucher expires today.

→ **Follow up #7** – after a further three days, we send them an email explaining that because we haven't heard from them we're assuming they no longer require this product.

→ **Follow up #8** – two days later they receive an email from me thanking them for giving us the opportunity to help them. I explain how, unless they object, they'll be getting regular emails from me just so if they do want to consider us again, they'll remember us.

→ **Follow up #9** – they're automatically added to my email nurturing campaign and they receive an email every working day for 30 days.

→ **Follow up #10** – they receive my daily emails until they buy, die or beg me to stop.

We know this works because we regularly convert prospects after one year, and sometimes even two, after they first enquired.

After sales campaigns

This is huge. Although I mentioned after sales campaigns in Chapter 3, I feel that it's such a huge way to grow your company's sales and profits that it deserves covering in depth here.

What really puzzles me is why most companies don't follow up after the sale and fail to realise how much easier it is to do more business with your existing customers than to gain new ones. It's also a lot cheaper too.

Not only does an after sales campaign help you build an even stronger rapport with your new customers, it also encourages them to buy more from you and helps you get more business by referrals.

Let's take a look at a six-stage after sales campaign that's very easy to automate and, once it's set up, takes little effort and hardly any of your time to manage.

Stage #1 Send an email thanking them for the business and ask them to complete a survey – All you need are five simple questions. Ask them to rate the service and products, whether they'd use you again, if they'd refer you to others and if there's anything they're looking for right now that you may be able to help with. Asking if they'd use you again and refer you subconsciously encourages them to do so.

If you're not customer facing (dealing directly with customers), make sure the email comes from the contact they know rather than from you. In the early days of my marketing efforts, my after sales campaign to new customers consisted of adding them to my daily email list. Suddenly they were receiving conversational daily emails from a total stranger. This resulted in them either unsubscribing or asking their contact, *"Who's that strange Mo guy who keeps sending me emails?"*

Stage #2 Send an introductory email – If your new customer doesn't know you, introduce yourself and let them know you'll be keeping in touch by email.

Stage #3 Send them a thank you gift – Two days after your introductory email, send them a thank you gift. Pop them a quick email to let them know they'll be receiving it in the next day or two. This helps them get used to receiving emails from you. Your gift doesn't need to cost much, but do make sure you have it decorated with your logo so they'll remember you, and don't forget to make sure it reflects quality, it's useful and it's not boring.

Stage #4 Send them an offer – Wait another two days and send them an email letting them know about another service or product you feel they'll benefit from. You could also offer them an incentive if they buy within a certain time. More for the same price or another extra you usually charge for. Don't forget your Call to Action; tell them exactly what they need to do to get it.

Stage #5 Ask them for a referral – Two days later, send them an email asking them to refer someone to you. Some people will refer you anyway, it's human nature to want to share an enjoyable experience, but by asking someone to, it'll increase the chances of them doing it and it will also remind them of the pleasure they felt when dealing with you. This will make them more likely to do business with you again.

Stage #6 Send them regular emails – It's easy for someone to forget you, so it's extremely important that you help them to remember you. Emails are the simplest and cheapest way to do it, but do remember to make them conversational, interesting and useful. Do remind them about your products and make them offers from time to time, but avoid a constant stream of boring sales emails, it's guaranteed to get them hitting the unsubscribe button.

Keeping hold of your existing customers

As we just covered, your after sales campaign will go a long way towards strengthening the rapport with your new customers and help them to remember you, but there's so much more you can and should do.

Before I walk you through the many simple strategies and tactics that'll help you achieve this, an email I sent to my list a while ago perfectly illustrates how much business companies are losing by failing to engage with their customers.

The scary facts behind why 68% of our customers stop buying from us

I've been looking at some stats about why people stop buying from businesses and it's actually quite scary.

Well, over two thirds of people stop buying from a company because of indifference, which could mean the after sales experience they've received didn't do much to make them feel valued.

Or it could be because the company doesn't keep in touch and someone you haven't heard from in a while is soon forgotten.

The reasons why people stop buying from businesses are:

- 1% die
- 3% move away
- 5% follow a friend or relative's recommendation
- 9% find an alternative they feel is better value
- 14% are dissatisfied with the products or services
- 68% stop buying from a business because of indifference

So things like sending a little thank you gift from time to time makes people feel you really do appreciate their business.

And generally, just keeping in touch as often as you can and by as many methods as you can think of, can be the difference between your customer or client choosing one of your competitors rather than you.

P.S. Mandy had a gem of an idea today, which we'll be including in the Club Row Chronicle. The only way to discover the idea for yourself is to register now.

Let's now look at a few ways you can stop 68% of your customers deserting you and ending up in the hands of your competitors.

→ **Send them a monthly newsletter**

We're talking here about a hard copy, land on your desk,

hold in your hand and read newsletter, rather than a bunch of links in an email that no one really reads because they look the same as all the other "newsletter" emails, which are actually no more than another poorly disguised, boring sales pitch. The huge advantage of a hard copy newsletter that you send in the post - compared to an e-newsletter - is that unlike emails that you can make disappear, something that lands on your desk has your complete attention.

So, how do you make your newsletter interesting and engaging?

There's a tried and tested formula that my mentor, Jon McCulloch, taught me. He learnt it by trial and error so it works better than most.

The most important thing is not to use your newsletter to sell your products, but to build your relationship with your customer. Give useful information, fun stuff that most people would enjoy reading and ensure that your personality flows through the entire copy. So, something like this...

30% Personal stuff (opinions and stories) – This is an opportunity to let people know a bit about you, your team and your company. Write about experiences you've had in business that people can learn from; issues you had and how you fixed them. I continue the story into the next month, which creates intrigue and keeps them wanting more.

20% Fun stuff (puzzles and things not relating to the thing you do) – People love to be entertained and get a break from work stuff in the office. This is a great opportunity to really get your personality across. Make the fun stuff about things you personally like. We have a quiz called 'Karissa's Krazy Kwiz'. Everyone who emails the correct answer is entered into a prize draw, and the winner receives a retail voucher for £50. We also have a monthly article called *"Mandy's Amazing Animal,"* because most of my team are huge animal lovers. This also helps to attract like-minded people.

30% About the thing you do (articles and teaching stuff) – Tell them about your products and the benefits of them. Have a featured product every month and offer a free sample or demo. You could have a tip each month relating to the thing you do. For example, if you're in the beauty industry, it could be simple tips to help keep your body trim.

What's really important is that you don't try and sell the thing you do. The purpose of your newsletter is to educate, entertain, engage them and keep your name in front of them.

20% About them (stuff that involves them) – Have a customer of the month feature. This is a great way to get your customers involved. The format we use for this is simple yet very effective. We ask them to send us a photo of themselves and tell us what problem they had and how we helped them solve it with our promotional products. Part of the article includes us talking about them and their company.

You'll find most of your loyal customers will be more than happy to help, and having them talking about you and your company in a positive way only helps to strengthen the relationship.

→ **Have prize draws**

We organise prize draws all the time, and we did three last year. The prizes our customers win total at least £1,000 every time.

Here's a question for you.

Why do you think having a free prize draw and giving away £1,000 worth of prizes and wanting nothing in return is such a good idea?

It's actually really easy to explain and something you really need to try yourself.

There are three reasons why having a free prize draw helps you keep hold of your customers, and it actually pays for the prizes 10 times over.

1. **You grab their attention** – Offering something for nothing makes them take notice. It helps them to engage with you and keeps them interested. In addition to your regular customers who use your products or services all the time, it also helps to bring back people who maybe haven't given you the chance in recent times and may have strayed into the path of your competitors. Keeping them engaged in this way makes them more likely to consider you when they next need the products or services you supply.

2. **If you give, you get something back** – It goes without saying that if you give something to someone or help them in some way without asking for something in return, they'll want to give you something back. It's how our brains are wired.

3. **They'll stay with you** – There's more chance they'll stay with you if you give them reasons to hang around.

   We always shoot a video to announce the winners, which means they'll actually hear us talking and see us doing stuff too. They're usually shot in our offices and are pretty amateurish, which shows we're normal and down to earth. This also helps them to get to know us a bit better.

→ **Invite them to a social event**

   This is the ultimate way to keep hold of your best customers and, if you pull it off, you really will keep hold of them forever.

   The best way to show you how this can work incredibly well is by way of a true story. It almost became the biggest disaster we'd ever been involved in, but we managed to rescue the situation and turned some of our best customers into raving fans.

   I'd toyed with the idea for quite a while of inviting our biggest and best customers to a curry night. We even suggested it to a few in passing and the general opinion was that the idea was great and they'd probably come along. I decided on a date, but then I backed down. I wasn't convinced they'd actually turn up and it could potentially turn into a PR nightmare. Imagine a curry night for 30 people and only two showing up?

   Then, a year or so later, we moved offices and that's when the idea came to me. I could combine a few things, which would include inviting everyone to my favourite curry house.

We'd call it the Coaching and Curry Day and we'd invite all our biggest and best customers to an afternoon at our new offices. They could meet the team and spend some time being shown how to get the best out of their promotional products. There would also be time to show them a few of our services and even have a quiz, just to lighten things up a bit. Then at the end of the afternoon we'd treat everyone to a curry.

We set the date, which was a few weeks after Christmas, towards the end of January. The invites went out just before Christmas and the number of people that said yes was... one.

There are two things I've learnt in life. There's no such thing as failure; if you try something and it doesn't go the way you expected, you haven't failed you've simply learnt something new. The second thing I've learnt is that if you want something badly enough and you're prepared to work hard at it, you'll get there in the end.

The thing I learnt from this was... the timing was wrong. It's almost impossible to get anyone so close to Christmas to commit to anything. All that's on their mind is the up-and-coming festivities. Also, people hardly ever respond to a request the first time you ask. So I changed the date and launched into a full-blown marketing campaign consisting of a series of emails and carefully scripted phone calls.

28 people accepted our invitation and the Curry and

Coaching Day was a resounding success. We strengthened our relationships, showed people how to make their promotional products work harder and better for them, and had a great evening together sharing a great curry.

Turning Your Customers into Raving Fans

Good customer service isn't important anymore.

When I say good customer service isn't important, what I mean is, we need to do more than just giving good customer service. Good customer service is the absolute bare minimum.

These days we need to turn our customers into raving fans.

A book I read recently called, funnily enough, *'Raving Fans'* by Ken Blanchard (which I highly recommend you get hold of), shows great examples of how you can wow your customers and turn them into raving fans.

Blanchard's three-step formula to getting *raving fans*:

Step 1: Decide what you want - First you need to have a vision of what will wow your customers and compare it to the way things actually are. So, simply list the different ways you look after your customers at the moment and then next to each one add something that's better or an additional action.

At this stage, it doesn't matter how crazy, over the top or impractical they are, you're just looking for some general ideas that will incur a reaction. It's also important to list the things

135

that would impress you, rather than second-guessing what would wow your customers. It's a bit trial and error – and testing your response will inevitably give you feedback with what works with your customers.

Here's an example from the book *'Raving Fans'* of the wow factor in action.

A guy goes into a bookshop to buy a book for his wife's birthday, which is the very next day. When he asks at the sales desk, the woman assistant tells him they're temporarily out of stock of the book he wants, but tells him if he's prepared to wait she'll buy a copy from another bookshop in the mall and have it gift wrapped and ready in 10 minutes. He accepts the offer and when he's ready to pay, the assistant charges him exactly what she paid (she doesn't charge extra for what she did). Most people simply don't get this but when you think about it, where will he go the next time he wants to buy a book and who will he recommend if someone asks for the name of a good bookshop?

Step 2: Discover what the customer wants - The obvious way to do this is simply to ask them, but there are three things you need to take into account when you do this.

1. **They say one thing and mean another** – people sometimes may think they mean one thing but they actually mean something completely different.

   A great example is when people say price is the most important thing to them. What they actually mean is value for money is important. When people go for the cheapest option and they're not happy with the quality, they never remember how much they paid, just the name of the supplier they used and why they should avoid them at all costs next time around.

2. **They don't expect a lot** – when you ask they just say fine.

Some people have low expectations when it comes to quality and service, so when you ask them how you did, they'll just say fine. They don't expect a service that is so good it takes their breath away. So if the service you give is just Ok and unremarkable, chances are they'll not remember you when they next need your products or services. Amazingly, outstanding service is something we should all deliver. Why? Because if you deliver a service that far exceeds their expectations, not only will they keep coming back, they'll tell others about you too.

3. **Silence** - they say nothing, they don't complain.

Funnily enough, most people don't complain enough or even at all. Many don't complain because they don't think it'll do any good. Some customers don't complain because they're worried it will negatively impact an otherwise good relationship. Instead, they silently take their business elsewhere or, even worse, they tell everyone they know, except you, about your poor service (and then take their business elsewhere).

So, discovering what your customers actually want needs to be a combination of what you know and feel, combined with what they tell you.

Step 3: Discover what the customer wants, plus one - So, you feel you've worked out exactly what you need to do to make your customers love you forever and throw money at you whenever they need your products or services.

Before I explain what is meant by plus one, I want to share a true story with you to show how sometimes we can get it completely wrong. It was probably about 20 years ago now that I came up with the great idea that every time we delivered an order to a customer, we needed to call them and ask if they were happy with the service they received.

Now, the idea was a good one but I must admit on one particular occasion my enthusiasm got the better of me and I messed up badly. It was a new customer and a few days after we delivered her T-shirts, I called her number. I was told she wasn't around and should try later. So, an hour later, I tried again and found she wasn't there. I left a message asking if she would call me and if I didn't hear from her I would call the next day. The next day arrived and I called her for a third time, only to be told she wasn't available. Now, I don't know why I did what I did next, but when I think back I realise what a ridiculously stupid thing it was to do. I said something along the lines of, "I really don't understand why she's refusing to speak to me, I just want to speak to her to make sure everything was Ok with her order and check she was happy with the service." I received an email later that day from my new customer telling me the T-shirts and service was fine but she'd never deal with us again.

So the lesson here is, learn by your mistakes and constantly look at improving the way you do things.

When you change the way you do things they don't always go the way you hope, so discover what the customer wants plus one means any changes you make should be in small, gradual steps. This means that if you do get it wrong you haven't gone completely in the wrong direction and can correct your course much easier.

The plus one also means plus 1%. Change can sometime be painful, but if you constantly look at improving the way you do things by just 1% a week, imagine what you'll achieve in a year.

The best and most moving example of outstanding customer service I've ever come across is best explained by one of my emails.

The man, the boy and the hotel

I read a story yesterday and I have no idea why, but something stirred inside, so much so that I want to share it with you.

Some say it's a true story and whether that's the case or not, it is certainly a powerful lesson in customer service, helping others and kindness and humanity.

Here it is exactly as I read it.

"A man and a young teenage boy checked into a hotel and were shown to their room.

The two receptionists noted the quiet manner of the guests, and the pale appearance of the boy.

Later the man and boy ate dinner in the hotel restaurant. The staff again noticed that the two guests were very quiet, and that the boy seemed disinterested in his food. After eating, the boy went to his room and the man went to the reception and asked to see the manager.

The receptionist initially asked if there was a problem with the service or the room, and offered to fix things, but the man said that there was no problem of that sort, and repeated his request.

The manager was called and duly appeared. The man asked to speak privately and was taken into the manager's office.

The man explained that he was spending the night in the hotel with his fourteen-year-old son, who was seriously ill, probably terminally so. The boy was very soon to undergo therapy, which would cause him to lose his hair. They had come to the hotel to have a break together, and also because the boy planned to shave his head that night, rather than feel that the illness was beating him. The father said that he would be shaving his own head too, in support of his son.

He asked that staff be respectful when the two of them came to breakfast with their shaved heads. The manager assured the father that he would inform all staff and that they would behave appropriately.

The following morning the father and son entered the restaurant for breakfast.

There they saw the four male restaurant staff attending to their duties, perfectly normally, all with shaved heads."

P.S. That really is a great example of going over and above what's expected of you when it comes to customer service, together with understanding and compassion.

Phew, that was a long chapter. However, I hope I've succeeded in showing you how easy it is to not only attract leads, but convert them into prospects, turn prospects into paying customers, encourage them to come back again and finally turn them into raving fans and customers for life.

KEY TAKE AWAY POINTS ARE:

✓ **Build the relationship before you start trying to sell to them** – You're much more likely to make the sale and keep them coming back again and again.

✓ **Follow up on a lead or prospect relentlessly** – The one that shows the most interest is more likely to get the business.

✓ **Keep in touch after the sale** – It's much easier to do more business with your existing customers than to gain a new customer. It's a lot cheaper too.

✓ **Good customer service isn't important anymore, it's the bare minimum expected** – Turn your customers into raving fans and you'll have them for life.

CHAPTER 7

The Consequences of Staying Still

Things change, and these days the speed of change happens at an incredibly fast pace. Although it's almost impossible to keep up with all the new technology and new ways of doing things, continuing to do the things in the same way will, for almost every business, result in failure and a collapse.

As new technology allows us to change the way we do things, it also changes our buying habits and expectations.

So, it's important to embrace change, realise that it ultimately makes our lives easier, understand that it allows us to do things we never could do before and that it improves the service we give to our customers. Let me give you a few examples of what I mean.

Things Can be Done Faster Than Ever Before

When we started out in business as T-shirt printers in the late 80s, personal computers were a thing of the future and fax machines were very expensive and hard to operate, so we relied heavily on the post and the telephone to communicate with customers and suppliers.

A quote would be sent by mail and followed up by a phone call a few days later. When an order was placed for printed T-shirts, the artwork or logo was sent to us either by courier or post.

These days, quotes are sent by email and can arrive in a matter of minutes. Orders are confirmed and artwork is sent just as fast. In the 80s and early 90s, the quickest turnaround for an order was two to three days, but now we can do it in less than 24-hours. Nowadays people expect and want things fast and are prepared to pay extra to get what they want.

Things Can be Done Now That Couldn't be Done Before

The emergence of the cloud has totally revolutionised the way we work. We're no longer chained to our desks and restricted to working in the office. We can log in anywhere in the world and recreate our 'office set up' remotely. This also means we're not restricted to employing people who are local, giving us the opportunity to take advantage of some of the best and most talented people from anywhere in the world.

In the past, small and medium-sized businesses would have been extremely limited in terms of the new tools they could use in their business because of the high costs of implementing the latest technologies. But the cheap, subscription-based delivery of cloud-based systems has meant that a company of any size can access the latest 'top of the range' products to help them grow their business.

The Service we Give Now Can be Better Than Ever Before

As I mentioned earlier, products can now be delivered faster than ever before and customers can be kept informed at every stage of the buying process. New technology also means we can communicate with our customers quicker, cheaper and more often, resulting in stronger relationships and greater loyalty.

In this chapter, I'll be covering the three stages of promotional product evolution: the past (how easy it was to get noticed using promotional products), the present (what you need to do to keep ahead of your competitors) and the future (what will happen if you don't keep up with new technology and changing buying habits).

The Past

The very first known promotional product can be traced back to 1789. In the United States, George Washington produced commemorative buttons when he was elected president.

Figure 17: George Washington's inaugural button

The earliest significant contributor to the promotional product industry was Jasper Freemont Meek. He owned a small newspaper business in Ohio and his incentive was to supplement his income by taking on print jobs between editions.

After seeing a child drop her schoolbooks in the dirt on Main Street, he came up with an idea that would create name recognition and ultimately increase sales. He approached his friend Mr Cantwell, owner of Cantwell Shoes, and persuaded him to imprint a book bag with a simple but direct message, *"Buy Cantwell Shoes"*. Cantwell gave every child who came into his shoe shop a free bag. The children would use the bag as they walked to and from school, so Cantwell's name would be seen all over town.

In the late 1950s, the promotional merchandise industry became established as a positive method of marketing here in the UK, and the real explosion of growth happened in the 1970s. The huge benefits of giving customers and prospects promotional gifts were realised and the industry grew from strength to strength. During that time, because it was a new and novel way to market a company, you didn't need to think too hard about what to give people and besides, available products and ideas were limited. So response rates were high and getting a good ROI was easy.

The Present

People's expectations are changing all the time and something like a cheap pen or keyring – which may have been gratefully received a few years ago - are ten a penny today, and not particularly appreciated or cherished. That said, some of these more basic products do still have their place, especially for the big corporates who focus heavily on building their brand and creating brand awareness by using the scattergun approach.

Also, as habits change and ways of doing things evolve, promotional products that once were useful and sought after have suddenly become out-dated. Bestsellers such as cigarette lighters, disposable one time use cameras and, more recently, car tax stickers have all ended up on the promotional product scrap heap - never to return again.

Promotional products are used in almost every marketing campaign these days and one approach you can adopt to help ensure the products you choose continue to stay effective and different enough to grab people's attention is to follow the AIDA principle. AIDA stands for Attention, Interest, Desire and Action. It's used in marketing and advertising to help develop successful communication strategies in a way that better responds to customers' needs and desires.

The AIDA Principle

A is for Attention – When creating copy for an email, sales letter, website page or direct mail piece, it's the subject or the headline that grabs people's Attention. Poster campaigns rely heavily on images with a compelling statement. One of the most successful poster campaigns of all time, which illustrates just how important an attention-grabbing headline is, was created for the Conservative Party by Saatchi & Saatchi as part of their 1978 election campaign. The poster showed a long queue of people outside an unemployment office, with the headline *"LABOUR ISN'T WORKING"*. It was widely accepted that the campaign helped the party win the election and Saatchi & Saatchi to grow into a global behemoth.

Figure 18: Labour isn't working poster campaign

An example of how promotional products can grab people's Attention involves the launch campaign in 1994 of the Orange mobile network provider. The campaign started with images of the Orange logo and the headline, *"The future's bright, the future's Orange"*. No mention was made about who they were or what they did; it was purely to get Attention. In addition to posters, adverts on the sides of buses and television advertising, they invested in thousands of sweatshirts, which they handed out bearing the logo and slogan. Before the launch, Orange was perceived as a 'lemon' in an overcrowded mobile network provider market. It quickly became a powerful brand and put a serious squeeze on market leaders, Cellnet and Vodafone.

I is for Interest – Once you have their Attention with your stop them in their tracks headline, picture or promotional product, you need to keep their Attention by creating Interest. Orange, for example, created intrigue in their launch campaign. All the initial advertising mentioned, *"The future's bright, the future's Orange,"* but they never actually said what Orange was or what Orange did.

Another way to create Interest is to offer something free. An award-winning hairdressers, when opening a new salon, carried out a direct mail campaign offering a free consultation or haircut and finish. This worked particularly well because the law of reciprocity also kicked in.

My very own Dream 100 campaign, which we covered in Chapter 4, is a great example of creating Interest. It's within the letter that accompanied the Zombie Juggling Balls. Following the brilliant (even if I say so myself) headline...

Don't Let Your Customers Think You're No Longer in the Land of the Living

...the opening paragraphs created the Interest...

You're probably looking at your set of Zombie Juggling Balls and wondering why anyone in their right mind would ever send you something so random and so odd.

So let me be totally honest and up front and tell you why...

D is for Desire – You now need to keep their Interest, and one of the most powerful ways to do this is to create Desire. One of the ways Orange created Desire in their launch campaign was through television advertising. One ad talked about the future and showed powerful images of how telecommunications was evolving into a future of clearer skies and a wire-free way of communication.

The award-winning hairdresser created the Desire by running exclusive local launch events close to the opening of the new salon. They also advertised in local press and social media, which created a buzz for people wanting an invite and excitement about seeing the new salon.

A is for Action – So now you have their Attention, Interest and Desire. The next bit, getting them to Do Something is critical, otherwise you'll lose them. A lot of marketing campaigns fall flat at this stage because the Call to Action is unclear or too complicated. So, your Call to Action should tell them exactly what you want them to do, why they should do it and what will happen next.

The *Call to Action* in the Orange television campaign was brilliant. First they mentioned how simple their billing procedure was compared to the confusing and complicated way all the other telecoms companies charged, and they also showed you exactly how much you'd pay each month. They then simply said, *"Call for a free brochure on..."*

The hairdresser also had a clear Call to Action. They advertised on Facebook with the simple request: *"Call to book"*.

Here's a great example of how, in 2006, Nintendo created a hugely successful marketing campaign using a promotional item to create awareness and increase sales of their game system.

Their objective was to assist the post-launch marketing and branding of their new Wii game system. The most unique feature of the Wii was the hand held remote console that let players interact with the game wirelessly. Taking advantage of this unique feature that differentiated it from their competition, Nintendo designed a keychain flashlight replica of the remote. Even the blue LED light was similar to the light on the real remote. They promoted the keychain on their websites as a free gift for new subscribers of the Nintendo Power Magazine, and it soon became the 'got to have' promotional item.

The results...

Immediately following the promotion, there was a distinct and significant increase in subscriptions to the Nintendo Power

Magazine. During the first period of the campaign, 130,000 key chains were sent out, with even more purchase orders submitted as demand increased.

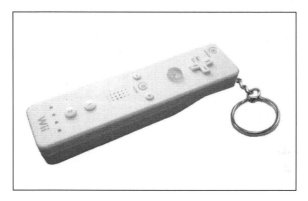

Figure 19: Wii flashlight keychain

The Future

I'd like to share some facts and figures with you. They are relevant and important in helping you to understand the future of the promotional products industry.

The total marketing spend in the UK is currently £33billion. In 2015, the promotional merchandise industry was valued at just under £1billion (£875,050,000 to be precise) and has been growing steadily at an average rate of around 4% each year since 2009, when the banking crisis of the previous year caused the market to decline.

The percentage of marketing budgets spent on promotional products is just 3%. In the US, promotional products represent 10% of marketing spend. This means that if the UK adopts the approach to marketing that they have in the US, and most things they do eventually influences the way we behave, marketing with the help of promotional products is set to continue an upward trend over the years to come.

Another indication this is likely is the fact that direct mail marketing is on the increase. As information online continues to grow, attention spans are dwindling. It's easier to simply hit delete when messages appear in your inbox than stop and read them, and surfing online for information has never been easier, which means grabbing someone's attention becomes more difficult. With direct mail, recipients are more likely to open your package, read the information and take Action. So, if your message is across both online and offline channels, the response will always be higher.

There will be two main changes to the way promotional products are used and benefited from over the next few years.

Promotional Products Will be Changing Faster Than Ever Before

As new technology moves faster, the types of promotional products needed to take advantage of the benefits will improve and change. Products that, because of new technology were bestsellers a few years ago, will become obsolete. Already we're seeing a huge decline in items such as mouse mats (because of the increased use of tablets and laptops) and USB flash drives (which is due to the growth in cloud-based systems).

This means that to keep ahead of competitors and stay fresh in the minds of your clients, it'll be even more important to be aware of new promotional products. Even fairly basic products that are unlikely to go completely out of fashion will alter as new technology and lifestyle changes give us more choice. Promotional T-shirts, for example, are now available in performance fabrics that can be manufactured more economically than they could 10 years ago. The quality of digital printing has moved forward in leaps and bounds, meaning we are less limited and can be more adventurous with the way we brand our promotional products.

These changes in the promotional products industry also mean the role of the supplier will change. Buyers are getting younger and will regularly purchase items online. The future role of the promotional product supplier will be as more of an advisor. Their focus will be more about understanding the buyer's needs and working with them to find promotional products that achieve the results they desire. Imagine having your own personal advisor, who understands your company, is familiar with your marketing campaigns and who gives you expert help and advice about products that'll give you the best ROI. Exceptional customer experience will be the order of the day.

Everything that can be, will be automated

Business Process Automation (BPA) is a systemised method that takes difficult, complex, repetitive and mundane tasks and simplifies them into a more streamlined and hands-free process.

As technology advances, more and more tasks will become automated. Tasks that only a decade ago we'd never have thought could be. For example, driverless cars are being tested and will be in use any day now. Tableside tablet ordering systems have already arrived at restaurants and may be in some casual dining establishments soon.

There are four main advantages to automation:

1. Saves time – Having the software or creating systems that can do things for you saves huge amounts of time. An example of this in my business is the use of training videos. In the past, I would physically sit with members of my team and show them how a new system or procedure worked. This not only required my time to train them, it also required time to answer questions and queries in the following days, while they got used to the new process. These days I simply shoot a video and send them the link.

2. Saves money – The obvious money saver is in staffing levels, but there are other ways that automation saves cash. Systematised procedures can avoid manual errors and inefficiencies that can be expensive to fix. An automated business process can ensure careless mistakes don't happen. Streamlining and automating your business processes will not only make your workforce more efficient, it will allow them to spend more time on their core areas of talent, ultimately leading to more business.

3. Makes things happen faster – Automated systems technology allows for faster processing of data and easier retrieval of information. A great example of this is how debit and credit card payments are made these days. When I worked in retail in the late 1970s, we had to take a physical impression of the card using a cumbersome machine that pressed the card against carbon paper and transferred the image onto a piece of paper. Today contactless payments are made in a matter of seconds.

4. Improves service – It goes without saying that by automating all the time-consuming and more mundane tasks, the service you give will improve enormously. You can send people the information they've requested in seconds or minutes rather than hours, freeing you to spend more time looking after customers. Our automated quotation system saves us the time it takes to manually follow up leads, which means we're able to spend more time with individual customers and understand their needs better.

Two examples of how automation will change the way we buy promotional products.

Personalised webshops

Webshops are a form of electronic commerce, which allows consumers or businesses to directly buy goods or services from a seller over the internet using a web browser. This system can be used in any industry where businesses need to reorder products on a regular basis. A personalised webshop allows regular customers to order their products fast, easily and at any time.

There are two main advantages of using a personalised webshop:

#1 Saves you time and hassle – Rather than the usual procedure of phoning or emailing, waiting for a response and then confirming your order, you simply log into your personalised webshop, click a few buttons and your items are ordered. Something that traditionally took a day or two now takes a minute or two.

#2 You can order anytime and you'll get it quicker – You don't have to order during office hours. You can place your order anytime, which means it's usually delivered two to three days earlier than usual (and sometimes up to a week).

Who will benefit?

Personalised webshops are not for everyone. There are costs involved to set one up, so if your annual orders total less than £3,000 and you don't order regularly, the financial and time-saving benefits are not necessarily cost effective.

We have a personalised webshop service for our preferred customers. If you'd like to know more about how you can become a preferred customer, go to the personalised webshops area of the website: www.promopowersupremacy.co.uk.

No minimum webshops

New technologies and advancements in digital printing have seen the emergence of totally automated e-commerce websites that allow you to choose your promotional products, add your logo or design, place your order and pay.

Personally I feel this method of buying promotional products has its downside.

Here's The Good, The Bad and The Ugly of no minimum webshops:

The Good – You can order anywhere and anytime and it will save you money. Because of digital technology you can order small quantities at relatively low cost, and the speed at which you can order and receive your promotional items is also much faster than the more traditional methods. Typically you'll receive your order in less than a week, which is the biggest advantage when you order low cost, basic promotional products.

The Bad – Unless you're familiar with the products you want to order, or you're an expert at buying promotional items, you'll be buying blind. Imagine walking into a clothes shop and buying a new outfit without trying it on and then a few days later, when you're ready to wear it, you realise it doesn't quite fit or look exactly how you imagined it would.

The Ugly – Ending up with something you're not happy with is a strong possibility when you buy something without seeing it first. It might look smaller than you thought it would, or the quality isn't quite what you expected. Alternatively, you may feel that your logo or design could have looked better.

GREAT LITTLE TIP

If the No Minimum Webshop method of buying is something you'd like to try, I suggest you allow yourself plenty of time and just order one to start with. If you're not happy with the final product, at least you'll be able to switch to something that suits you better. It's better to be disappointed with one item than 100 items.

So there you have it. Things are changing faster than ever before and I've no doubt they will continue to do so. Although change is good and all the new things coming our way will be a huge benefit to our companies and personal experiences, there is one caveat. The focus must always be on the changes that make our customers' experiences better and more enjoyable rather than to save money or time. Having a call centre, for example, in a developing country whose staff are not at ease with our language may save money, but could frustrate customers and push them into the arms of competitors.

KEY TAKE AWAY POINTS ARE:

✓ **Embrace change** – Let new technology help you constantly change and improve the ways you do things.

✓ **Promotional products will be changing faster than ever before** - This means it'll be even more important to be aware of new promotional products if you want to keep ahead of your competitors.

✓ **The AIDA principle** – This process will help you create highly successful marketing campaigns, but don't forget that your Call to Action needs to be clear and simple.

✓ **Automation will be key** – Use new technology to automate your business to free up time, save money, speed up processes and improve service.

CONCLUSION

You now have everything you need to choose your promotional products in a way that is better, quicker, easier and involves less hassle but, more importantly, you know how to make your promotional products work harder and give you a much higher and measurable ROI.

There is a lot to take in and plenty you can do, so let's make it a bit easier for you by having a look at the top four key points, followed by a few little tips to help you along the way.

Key point #1 – You need never fail again

We covered in Chapter 1, *The 7 Reasons Why Promotional Products Fail Miserably in Most Cases, and How to Fix That*, so now you're armed with everything you need to avoid wasting money.

If you don't remember them all don't worry for now, the most important things you need to memorise are the *3 Golden Rules.*

Golden rule number 1 – The products you choose must ooze quality, but that doesn't mean you need to spend a fortune.

Golden rule number 2 – Make sure the product is useful. It's the usefulness of the item, not its perceived cost, that matters most.

Golden rule number 3 – Make it different. Avoid boring. If the product is different it will get noticed, remember the gold-coloured mints?

Key point #2 – The motives for investing in promotional products

Be very clear why you're spending money on promotional products and make sure the products you choose are relevant. The scattergun approach of investing in a few thousand plastic pens and handing them out to all and sundry in the hope it creates awareness is a bit like throwing seeds in the air in the hope the wind blows them onto fertile ground. It's not going to happen.

Decide what you want to achieve, who your target audience is and then select the products that'll give you the best chance of success.

Key point #3 – Investing in promotional products is not a quick fix

In Chapter 5, we looked at promotional products in action, and the benefits are not always measured in terms of immediate hard-earned cash.

Jan's awareness campaign, for example, was to promote her weekend ice skating disco sessions. Her promotional logo torch keyring created such a buzz amongst teenagers that the Riverside Ice & Leisure Centre became the coolest place in town.

Part of Mark's staff retention campaign was to hand out specially printed T-shirts to everyone at his team bonding trips. This helped to make staff feel important and have a sense of belonging. Although his success is difficult to quantify in terms of cash saved, his record of having one of the highest staff retention rates of any BPO in the Philippines says it all.

Key point #4 – Automation is key to your success

If you haven't automated at least some of your processes and systems, you are being left behind, and if you don't start automating soon you will struggle to keep up with your competitors and business will start to seriously suffer.

Back in 1989, when my company was barely two years old, we commissioned a consulting company to carry out an audit of our business. We wanted to know what we needed to do to grow. The one big thing the report said was this...

> *"The fax as a method of communication is the future and any business that doesn't use fax as their main method of communication will not be around in six months' time."*

So I'd like to say to you: *"Automating your systems as a method of communication is the future and any business that doesn't will struggle to keep ahead."*

Just do it

So, what are you going to do now? I've shared everything I know about promotional products and the tried, tested and proven strategies that you can put to work in your company.

All you need to do now is start using the information. But it's one thing to read and know what you need to do, and another to actually do it. When people read books, or learn new strategies for their business, only 1% of people will use and implement that information. Be one of the 1%.

None of the stuff you've learnt will work unless you take action, and one of the reasons I've written this book in the way I have is to make it as easy as possible for you to start implementing straightaway.

Ok, I understand it's not as simple as that. It's in our nature to shy away from stuff we haven't done before. We worry that maybe we won't be able to do it - a kind of fear of failure kicks in which makes us put it off.

Here's an email I sent to my list a while ago that will help explain why we fear doing new stuff...

The devil on your left shoulder

You get this amazing idea; it's so good you just wonder why you didn't think of it before.

It's so obvious you're surprised someone else didn't think of it first. You want to get started straightaway because you don't want the same thing to happen as last time when you left it and then saw something that made you say to yourself, "Hey, that's my idea, I thought of it first!"

You start working on your new idea and you realise that although it's simple, it's actually not that easy, and that's when it starts...

You hear a sound in your ear coming from your left shoulder, "Hey {FIRST_NAME}, it's not going to work, give up, you're wasting your time. Why put yourself through all this?"

Then you hear another voice, but this time it's coming from your right shoulder. "Don't listen to him {FIRST_NAME}, you can do this and you know it'll work, just push through this and it'll start to get easier."

That's when in your heart you know you need to keep going and even if your idea doesn't work as well as you hoped it would, you'll learn from it and other things will develop from it.

And at least you can say to yourself, *"I had an idea, it was all mine. I tried, I followed it through and I've learnt from it."*

We all have a devil on our left shoulder and he's always trying to stop us doing things we know we should do, things we know are right. Sometimes it's easier to listen to him than the angel on our right shoulder. He's the one we know we really should be listening to.

So, if you have an idea, stick with it, listen to the angel whispering in your right ear and have the courage to keep going.

Theodore Roosevelt said: "Courage is not having the strength to go on; it is going on when you don't have the strength."

And finally, this is a great way to help you to start implementing everything I've told you...

How to tackle the hard stuff

When we're faced with 101 things to do, be them difficult but exciting new strategies, or mundane routine procedures, we generally choose the easy stuff, just to get them out of the way, and then we choose a few other easy things after that, just to get them out of the way, and then we're ready to start on the difficult things we really need to be doing, but...

... By then it's late in the afternoon, we're feeling a bit tired, our brain's not working as well as it was first thing so we decide to make those things a priority tomorrow.

Problem is, when tomorrow comes the same thing happens and the thing that really needs doing gets put to one side.

So here's what works for me.

Pick the hardest thing on your list and just start doing it. The difficult thing is making a start, but once you've started, it's surprising how easy it suddenly all becomes.

And then when you've completed that task it will spur you on to do more and more. Before you know it, you've achieved more than you ever imagined you could.

Most people's brains work best first thing in the morning before fatigue starts to slow things down so, doing the more demanding things early means you can easily deal with the rest later in the day.

So, armed with all of this information, it's time to get started! I wish you all the best, and please let me know how you get on with these strategies and tactics. Just email me... I look forward to hearing from you.

Mo Yusuff

NEXT STEPS

So, you now have everything you need to make your promotional products work harder for you.

Having said that, if you'd like some extra help, visit the website: <u>www.promopowersupremacy.co.uk</u>

You'll not only find the specific resources mentioned in the book, but if you register, I'll send you some additional tips and tricks to help you along the way.

Not just that...

I'll also send you a free example of a great promotional product that ticks all the boxes. (Remember my comment on page 39 about grabbing yourself a free sample?)

And there's even more...

I'll also be there for you, so if ever you get stuck or need some friendly, helpful advice, I'll be there to help you every step of the way. If you know me, you'll be aware that I seldom take calls and rarely work personally with customers, but because you've read my book, I want you to benefit from it and give you everything you need to do it, so you'll get the opportunity to speak to me about anything you'd like help with.

A quick word of warning...

Simply reading the book will not give you the results you deserve, you need to get stuck in and start doing stuff now while it's fresh in your mind. The longer you delay the harder it'll become, so take action now.

Simply visit the website and add your details:
www.promopowersupemacy.co.uk

I look forward to seeing you on the site.

ABOUT THE AUTHOR

Mo Yusuff realised when he worked part-time in a menswear shop that clothing was his passion. He left college and worked full-time as a sales assistant, working his way up to shop manager for a menswear retail company.

His ambition to become a fashion buyer was realised when he joined Debenhams as a trainee. He rose through the ranks and became the youngest senior buyer in the menswear buying team.

Following his successful eight-year career at Debenhams, Mo started his own business in 1987. With three friends, he bought a T-shirt printing machine and began designing and printing fashion T-shirts for companies such as Top Man, Freemans Mail Order, C&A and Reiss. Then, in 1987, Mo's company was approached by ITV to supply promotional clothing for their bi-annual telethon. He naively guaranteed delivery of all orders within seven days, not realising at the time that the demand would be for tens of thousands of T-shirts every week for six months. He kept his promise, which led to supplying other large companies with promotional clothing. Soon after that he was asked to supply items such as pens, mugs and key chains. It seemed the most obvious direction to take the business in, and Mo's team began to build their new range of promotional products.

His extensive training at Debenhams taught Mo everything there is to know about high-quality products and this has followed him throughout his career.

Mo is Managing Director of Club Row Creations, one of the leading promotional product companies in the UK. He lives in London with his partner Nikki and he loves travelling to The Philippines, where he has a second home.

ACKNOWLEDGEMENTS

To Mandy Jubb, my best friend, for putting up with all my ridiculous ideas in both my business and personal life over the last 30 years.

To Nikki Gerodias, my partner, whose words, "Go on, Boom Boom, I know you can do it," helped me enormously when I was struggling to write.

To my mentor, Jon McCulloch, for teaching me everything I know about marketing and copywriting.

To my Elite Mastermind business group for bullying me into writing this book.

And to Alexa Whitten, my book coach, for helping me to get this book written.

RESOURCES

Robert Cialdini – *Influence: The Psychology Of Persuasion*

Chet Holmes – *The Ultimate Sales Machine*

Jon McCulloch – *Grow Your Business Fast*

Ken Blanchard – *Raving Fans*